Orma Lee Mac
641 Empire Drive
Ukiah, Ca.
phone 463-2225

OVERCOMING
DEPRESSION

Richard King Mower, Ph.D.

Deseret Book

Salt Lake City, Utah

No part of this book may be reproduced in any
form or by any means without permission in writing
from the publisher, Deseret Book Company,
P.O. Box 30178, Salt Lake City, Utah 84130

First printing February 1986

Library of Congress Cataloging-in-Publication Data

Mower, Richard King, 1954–
   Overcoming depression.

   Includes index.
   1. Spiritual life—Mormon authors.   2. Depression,
Mental—Religious aspects—Christianity.   I. Title.
BX8656.M69   1986   248.4'8933206   85-29228
ISBN 0-87579-025-9

CONTENTS

FOREWORD

It is with interest and pleasure that I write a foreword to a book such as this. In my eleven years of work in mental health settings, I have been fortunate enough to counsel extensively with Latter-day Saint patients. Many members of the Church seek treatment from a professional only after they have tried prayer, blessings, administrations, and fasting to solve their problems. These approaches are often effective, but sometimes underlying issues reemerge and the old problems return. When this happens, the individual may wonder why the Lord allows problems to come back. It has become clear to me, however, that He will not always insulate or isolate us from the trials inherent in this mortal existence. Without trials, we would not move forward in our attempts to overcome, and to eventually become as He is.

This book, which I heartily endorse, contains a set of tools or ideas that a Latter-day Saint can use in his progression out of depression into a richer life. In my experience, after three years of developing and teaching seminars using many of these ideas, I have learned that people select the combination of tools that works best for them. Most of the material in this book comes from contemporary research, theory, or clinical experience in the treatment of depression. Dr. Mower and I have spent hours exchanging and refining some of the ideas. He has also included some material that is unique to his own experience.

Members of the Church can easily become dissatisfied with approaches suggested in modern psychology literature if they expect these ideas to be the final answer. But if these approaches are viewed as handy tools containing some truths to be used in perfecting oneself in an incremental way, then the proper perspective is maintained. Psychology is *not* like scripture. It never arrives at its fullness. It is a product of fallible human beings. Twenty years from now we will probably know more about depression, and we will probably be able to say much more in a book about how to overcome depression.

The thirteenth Article of Faith states, "If there is anything . . . of good report or praiseworthy, we seek after these things." In the context of attempts to better ourselves and overcome opposition, this book is both praiseworthy and of good report. The concepts given here can be very helpful in dealing with depression. I have personally seen many individuals who were seriously depressed use these ideas to facilitate their own self cure.

Edwin R. Christensen, Ph.D.
Psychologist

PREFACE

This book was written in response to two observations from my clinical practice: that people are generally unaware of new strategies available to help overcome depression, and that members of The Church of Jesus Christ of Latter-day Saints are often reluctant to seek help for their psychological problems because of fear that the counsel they receive will run counter to their religious values. By writing a book based on current psychological theory and practice from the philosophical viewpoint of LDS teachings, I have sought to break through both of these barriers and create a bridge between psychology and theology.

I want to acknowledge the contributions of Edwin R. Christensen, Ph.D., for assisting me in conceptualizing the book and freely sharing his ideas and experiences; J. Courtney Black, Ph.D., for providing needed encouragement to finish the project as well as co-writing the chapter on perfection; and Linda Charney, Ph.D., for her review of the manuscript and helpful suggestions. Finally, but most importantly, I express my gratitude to my wife, Mary Ann, for her editing, proofreading, typing, and enthusiasm for this project, as well as to the rest of my family for their support and encouragement.

INTRODUCTION

It came on suddenly. We had just moved and were settling down in our new house. One morning I felt really blue, and each day it got a little worse. At first I wanted to sleep all the time; then I stopped being able to sleep. I was tired and didn't want to do anything. I felt guilty. I stopped playing tennis; even that didn't seem like much fun. Then one day the Spauldings stopped by. Clark played tennis and asked me to join him. I started to think, 'Hey, I've moved before and it wasn't the end of the world. I really do like our new neighborhood.' Now I'm feeling much better. I guess I was just depressed."

Depression is a confusing word because it is used to describe a broad range of feelings, from disappointment, to "being down in the dumps," to not caring if we live or die. Depression is diagnosed by professionals from a number of emotional and behavioral symptoms that usually, but not always, include the following: loss of interest or pleasure in almost all activities; "blue" mood with feelings of sadness or hopelessness; change in appetite or weight; changes in sleep patterns; thoughts of death or suicide; loss of energy; feelings of worthlessness; diminished ability to think or concentrate; and agitation or retardation of motor behavior (movements of the body). Those who are depressed do not suffer from all of these symptoms all of the time. The number of symptoms experienced and the severity of the symptoms vary from person to person and can change over time within each person.

Depression is a common problem. Although some people are more susceptible than others, everyone can get depressed. Depression is the most frequently diagnosed psychiatric illness in the United States, cutting across all walks of life: rich and poor, religious and non-religious, old and young. Each year one in ten adults will experience an episode of depression. Some researchers have estimated that up to 50 percent of the population is likely to experience moderate to serious symptoms of depression at some time during their lifetime, and at least 5 percent of the people in the United States would fit the most rigorous diagnostic criteria for depression at any given time. Recently it has been speculated that members of The Church of Jesus Christ of Latter-day Saints experience depression more often or more intensely than the general population because of theological or cultural mores, such as the promotion of large families, the idea that women should remain in the home, or an insistence on high performance standards. Current studies indicate, however, that neither Latter-day Saint men nor Latter-day Saint women are more or less at risk than non-Mormons.

Everyone will experience symptoms of depression from time to time. Our moods are actually best understood as moving back and forth along a continuum, with depression at one end and euphoria at the other. Mood changes occur from day to day in everyone.

The probability that one may develop depression varies for each individual. Some important factors have been identified that indicate when the risk increases: losses or changes in life; a lack of intimate relationships;

a history of past experiences with depression; and the occurrence of depression in other family members.

Losses and changes in life appear to be frequent precursors of depression. Death, marital separation, serious physical illness, financial problems, and friends moving to another city are all examples of changes. A job promotion, starting a strict new diet, moving to a new home, the birth of a child, returning to work, even a new church calling can precede depression, even though they are positive steps in one's life. Any change has the potential to precipitate depression because change requires us to move away from our old ways of thinking or doing things. As we break up old patterns, we often experience some degree of frustration while we're learning to adapt to the change. This frustration and confusion can lead to depression. Not every change or loss produces depression, but it is one of many factors that can signal increased vulnerability.

The lack of intimate relationships often contributes to the development of depression. Those who have a close confidant, particularly a spouse or steady boyfriend or girlfriend, are less likely to become depressed when faced with losses or changes in their lives. The depth of the relationship rather than the frequency of the contact appears to be the most important factor in alleviating depression.

Past symptoms of depression increase the probability of future occurrences. Both biological and behavioral explanations have been advanced to explain this tendency. For instance, there is some evidence that depression runs in families through biological or genetic causes. This does not mean that in a family where one person is depressed, everyone will become depressed, however. It is not yet fully understood why some members of families where depression occurs maintain more normal moods.

The scriptures tell us that "Adam fell that men might be; and men are, that they might have joy." (2 Nephi

2:25.) Joy, peace, and happiness are God's wish for us in this life. We can attain joy in many ways: by remaining faithful to the commandments, enjoying family and friends, experiencing success in our careers or pleasure from hobbies. There are also times when we may experience depression or despair, even if we are trying to keep the commandments of our Heavenly Father. Joseph Smith expressed this feeling eloquently while he was imprisoned in Liberty Jail (see Doctrine and Covenants 121). Depression is not a punishment for unrighteousness or lack of zeal in the gospel. It also cannot always be relieved by resolving conflicts between one's current lifestyle and the commandments. Everyone has hard times because this life is a mixture of pleasure and pain, and an opportunity to learn how to enlarge ourselves and transcend our troubles.

Professionals in mental health have struggled for years to develop ways to help those who are depressed. Early treatments focused on trying to discover what might be people's unconscious reasons for staying depressed or identifying past experiences they had that promoted patterns of depression. These forms of therapy met with only limited success. Other therapists encouraged patients to express their feelings, particularly anger, which was viewed as a chief cause of depression. The idea was that depression is anger toward others that is instead turned toward ourselves. Having the person express these feelings offered initial relief, but long-term positive changes often did not occur. There have been many other remedies prescribed for depression, from "go somewhere and cry it out" to "just forget it." Current research has identified four core areas that affect depression: (1) thoughts and ways of thinking; (2) daily enjoyment of the world around us; (3) relationships with other people; and (4) physical health, including the use of medications. Successful strategies for dealing with issues in these areas have also been developed.

This book will discuss these critical areas from which

depression may develop and present various strategies for overcoming depression and increasing joy. Think of it as a cookbook that allows you to identify those areas that are most important to you and the techniques you are most comfortable using to initiate changes in your life. Each individual will have his own needs and "tastes" and, therefore, will develop his own menu. Please sample each of the chapters to expand your available repertoire of options. Frequently a combination of work in each area is necessary to alleviate symptoms of depression.

The techniques described in this book have been proven effective in decreasing depression of all types, from the occasional bout with the blues to serious clinical depression. Many people are surprised at the simplicity of some of the techniques, but researchers have repeatedly established the power of these tools. The professional counselor's challenge is often to convince patients to initiate programs for change. With persistence and work, depression can be controlled.

One of the common beliefs of depressed people is that they have no alternatives to their depression, but actually, it is possible for everyone to achieve more joy from life. Just reading the ideas in this book will not make much difference, though; this would be like reading a recipe and then expecting to feel your hunger satisfied. Taking some action to change your current circumstances will be necessary. Though we all wish for instant solutions to the problems of life, there are no shortcuts to happiness; it is a reward that follows honest efforts.

Chapter 1

AS WE THINK, SO WE ARE

For several years psychotherapists and others have been encouraging the public to express their feelings, tune in to themselves, and "let it all hang out." Many schools of therapy have taught that the truest sense of self actually resides in an individual's inner feelings, and the best way to "mental health" is to let those feelings out. Since feelings have been a predominant focus of professionals, we have become accustomed to hearing choices explained in the language of feelings: "I just don't feel like hamburger tonight," "he always felt as if his father didn't like him," "I felt like hitting her." As we listen to ourselves and to others, it is easy to begin to believe that feelings are the cause of most reactions and decisions, but where did these feelings come from?

Perhaps a few of our feelings are accounted for by genetics and actually existed before birth. For instance, babies seem to be more interested in human faces or even cards or balloons with faces drawn on them than in any other object. They respond with actions and sounds that indicate pleasure, such as cooing or looking toward the face. They lose interest, however, if the eyes, nose, or mouth are rearranged or out of place. They seem to know innately how faces are supposed to look. Infants also respond to loud noises and abrupt movements with signs of distress, such as crying. Although there may be a few other feeling-like responses present from birth, they do not explain the great diversity of attitudes and tastes of mankind. They don't explain the "feeling" that we didn't want asparagus last Tuesday, or that we do or do not like opera, or that some people "feel" better about going to the dentist than others.

Current research indicates that our thoughts create the great diversity in feelings that we experience. Thoughts give meaning to experience by organizing information received in the brain and directing the body to react. Feelings are an emotional response to thoughts. For example, imagine this scene: You are standing under the only light on a very dark street as a figure begins to approach from the darkness. The light first catches the face, which appears ashen, almost colorless, with sunken eyes and hideously deformed features. The figure seems to be coming straight toward you. If your thoughts remind you that today is Halloween, you might not feel any apprehension. On any other day, however, you would probably feel afraid. The thought that "today is Halloween" mitigates the fear.

Though our eyes and ears receive information about the world around us, it is the brain and its thoughts that differentiate between our mother's voice or that of a stranger. Thoughts place sensory experiences in perspective by assigning meaning to life. Controlling thoughts, then, is the first step in effectively dealing with feelings. For example, were you just thinking of pink elephants? Now you are because I suggested it. Images are created and feelings aroused by thoughts. If you are still not convinced about the connection between thoughts and feelings, try this experiment. Divide a small group of people into two sections and ask those in one section to close their eyes. Write the words *pear, apple,* and *peach* on a piece of paper or chalkboard for the others to see. After erasing or hiding the words, have the groups reverse roles. Show the second group these words: *knot, lasso,* and *lariat.* After removing these words, ask both groups to open their eyes. Hold up a sign or write on the board R_PE, and ask members of the groups to fill in the missing letter. The first group will answer RIPE, the second group ROPE. Their thoughts have been influenced because of the differences in the messages they received. One group thought about fruits, the other about uses for rope. We can learn to control the direction of thoughts in this way, by preparing our minds to interpret information in a positive and constructive manner.

Because feelings are affected by so many variables and are unique and idiosyncratic to each of us, they are not the most reliable information to use in interpreting what is happening around us. Decisions based only on feelings are subject to many distortions because feelings are often remnants of a past experience or former ideas that may no longer be relevant. For example, Mary was enjoying a potluck dinner with some refugees she was teaching. She particularly liked one Southeast Asian delicacy and asked what it was. When she learned it was fried pigs' ears, she felt nauseated. The fact is that she enjoyed the dish, but she allowed her emotional reaction to the idea of "pig's ears" to overrule the reality that she had been enjoying them.

Feelings can serve as signals and provide information about initial reactions, but they may not represent a realistic view of the situation. Most people have experienced getting carried away by emotions at times when their extreme reaction was not appropriate to what was really going on. Everyone makes mistakes and misjudges situations. Depressed people are, however, more likely to believe their feelings without questioning their validity or rationality. They avoid thinking rationally about situations and assume that because they feel depressed, their experiences in life are really negative. Letting the heart rule the head often ends up in heartache, however. We need to challenge feelings and allow for the possibility that they may be based on faulty information or irrational thoughts. If we do so, we will open the door to more positive attitudes and greater happiness in life.

Automatic Thoughts

As adults, we are involved in many activities that have become fairly automatic, such as driving a car, using sophisticated machinery, or sewing. There was a time, however, when these tasks were difficult and required complete concentration to do them correctly. Try to recall when you were learning to drive or type or play a musical instrument. It takes a while to learn to change chords on a guitar without looking at your finger placement, but with practice these changes begin to feel more natural. Typists don't have to think through each finger movement—hands on home base and away they go. Many things have become automatic to each of us, including the patterns of our thoughts.

A piece of folk wisdom states that optimists will say a glass is half full while pessimists will say it is half empty. Some people have developed the habit of seeing a dark side to almost everything and can find a cloud for every silver lining. Depressed individuals automatically distort or change their thoughts about what actually happens to fit a generally gloomy picture. They assume the worst from others and expect the worst for themselves and may not realize that these attitudes are actually the result of a pattern of thinking that has developed over many years.

Thought patterns begin very early in life. A child's conscience, one form of automatic thinking, develops from teachings of parents and other early experiences. For instance, a four-year-old tells his friend, "We don't jump on beds at our house; my daddy doesn't like it," even though he really wants to do it. Parental rules will eventually become the core of the normal child's conscience, as a result of years of exposure to them. The injunction not to jump on the bed will begin to feel like a natural part of the older child's internal values. For some people, however, this healthy process is twisted, and a tyrannical, critical, perfectionistic inner self develops that seems to automatically control their thoughts, color their perceptions, and contribute to their chronic depression.

Debbie, a divorcée, had gone through her life with just this kind of despotic inner voice. As an adult she had been in a series of relationships with people who were desperately unhappy themselves and took advantage of her. If she stood up to them, thoughts like these went through her mind: "You're just selfish. You're a 'meanie.' You think only of yourself." She traced the origin of these thoughts to her early life, when she had been told repeatedly that it was selfish to assert her own needs or set limits on the demands of others. If there was a disagreement within her family, she was expected to give in and was called a "meanie" if she did not. These early criticisms became automatic thought patterns, limiting her ability to interact in a healthy way with others.

Automatic thoughts are similar to the body's muscle reflexes. Many muscle reflexes do not require the brain to process information or make decisions before the body responds. For example, a doctor's hammer striking the knee causes a reflexive kick before the brain receives information about the sensation or determines what to do next. In a similar manner, the thinking of some people develops a negative inner reflex that is just as automatic. Reactions take place automatically, before they can even think about them, causing thoughts about themselves and the world around them to be grotesquely misshapen.

Some kinds of automatic thoughts or thought distortions are common to depressed people. Four of these destructive distortions can be remembered easily by using the mnemonic (memory aid) *L-O-S-E:* Labeling;

Omniscience, Omnipotence, and Overgeneralizing; Shoulds; and Extremes. Thoughts can be reanchored in reality and depression decreased by uncovering these distortions, challenging their validity, and refusing to respond in the old automatic way. Consider your own thoughts as you read, and try to identify those distortions that may influence your own moods.

Labeling

Think for a moment about poor Charlie Brown. His friends in the *Peanuts* comic strip call him a "blockhead," and he thinks of himself as a blockhead, too. I assume that being a blockhead means he is stupid, but I have found him to be quite insightful at times. For instance, he clearly understands that Lucy will not hold the football while he kicks it; he just wants to believe he can trust her (perhaps it is *her* character that is flawed, not his). We know that Charlie Brown is good to his sister and loyal to his dog. There is really much to admire about Charlie, but he believes he is a blockhead anyway. It would be hard to convince him he is not.

Like Charlie Brown, our first experiences with labels are usually as children, when we begin to use them to categorize the many varieties and subtleties we observe in the world around us. Because of these early attempts at labeling, going to the zoo with a two-year-old can be entertaining; anything with four legs is a "doggy," "kitty," or "horsey." Children are very enthusiastic about skunks and tigers, because they believe they are just kitties.

Luckily, as adults we become more discriminating and sophisticated with our labels—or do we? Have you ever not completed a task on time, burned dinner, or not anticipated what your friend really wanted? Those who are vulnerable to depression are likely to say "I'm a failure" or some derivative of that label in these situations. Clearly they are not failures—they did finish the task or have finished other things, dinner is not always burned, and they can, at times, please their friends. What is a failure, after all? It is only one of those tragic labels, superficial shorthand that describes everything yet nothing, everyone and no one. Everyone has failed from time to time, but I have yet to meet a real failure.

Labeling ourselves and others is harmful and deceptive. Most people become accustomed to hearing labels about themselves and labeling others very early and never stop to consider the consequences. Unfortunately, labels can become as predictive as they are descriptive as we limit our choices in life based on old misperceptions. Consider the labels you gave yourself or others gave you while you were growing up: "tomboy," "jock," "egghead," "wallflower," "busybody," "cynic," "sweet spirit," "slob," "emotional wreck," "showoff," "underachiever," "introvert." Write your labels down on a piece of paper and see how well they describe you. Typically they reflect only a few events in life and a very narrow perspective.

Just as we discovered that failure doesn't really describe anyone, you'll probably agree that your own labels are mostly inaccurate and generally useless. They don't tell the whole story or offer a balanced picture of how you really are. Labeling distorts reality; people are not fixed and stagnant objects or things, but unique characters on an ever-changing stage. Labeling is like describing a cross-country drive by telling of one stop along the way.

The story about the blind men and the elephant teaches an important lesson about labeling. Six men, blind from birth, took pride in their wisdom and wanted to learn about elephants. The first man bumped into the elephant's side and declared that an elephant was like a wall. The second, after grasping a tusk, described the elephant as something like a spear. The third touched only the trunk and was sure an elephant was similar to a snake. The other three, after touching the elephant in different places, exclaimed it must be like a tree, a fan, or a rope. All accurately described the part of the elephant they had handled, but they missed understanding what it really was altogether.

Labels make us blind to the "elephant" as a whole and describe only part of the actual picture. Depressed people distort reality by negatively labeling one facet of themselves or others and then believing their label represents an accurate picture. This, of course, often deepens their depression.

Clearing your thoughts and speech of destructive labels is an important goal to work toward. There are some steps you can take immediately to reduce their use. First, try to deal only in the present with criticism; then link it to a specific event; and finally, don't exaggerate. For example, "You're a slob" can become "Please pick up your toys; I feel angry when I see them on the floor." "I'm a loser" becomes "I'm disappointed because I lost the Evans' account," or "I'm a pig" becomes "I ate too much ice cream last night." Statements that avoid labeling require that we be specific and accurate in describing a situation. This provides helpful feedback instead of fostering a cycle of recriminations or name calling, which undermines self-esteem. It also leaves room for others to change or respond to our wishes rather than creating defensiveness in them and depression in ourselves.

Though it is clear that labeling is destructive, it can still be a hard habit to break. Here are some additional suggestions to decrease the negative affects of labeling:

1. Look again at the list of labels you generated earlier, and be prepared to reject them if they reappear in your thoughts. Replace them with a positive, accurate statement about yourself.

2. As labels occur in your thoughts, write them down and then respond realistically. Deal only in the present, linking criticism to a specific event, and don't exaggerate.

3. Ask someone you frequently spend time with, such as your spouse, a friend, or a co-worker, to help you

become aware of any labeling they may hear you do. Replace labels by using positive communication skills such as those mentioned above. With some effort and concentration you'll get good results.

Omniscience, Omnipotence, and Overgeneralizing

Children and young adults experience two common fantasies: (1) they can control or predict what will happen in the future, and (2) they are the center of the universe with all decisions and actions revolving around them. Theologians refer to these qualities as omniscience and omnipotence, abilities attributed to deity. Mental health professionals call these fantasies "magical thinking" in children, but in adults they become black magic, and the magician becomes the victim of his own thoughts. For instance, believing that he already knows what people are thinking, the pseudo-magician refuses to check out with others his assumptions about what their words or actions mean, and he makes decisions based on his distorted view of reality. At other times he may try to predict the future based unrealistically on unrelated past performances or on his attitude about himself. He thereby becomes excluded from opportunities for growth and happiness. It would be a heady feeling to possess these powers, but it is really a very destructive fantasy. Belief in our own omniscience and omnipotence leads to the assumption that our experiences or feelings are true in every instance. We then overgeneralize by taking a little information and drawing broad conclusions. Let's examine a few of the ways these mistaken ideas create havoc and contribute to depression.

Mind reading is both a fascinating and a fear-provoking possibility. Several popular books have been written recently purporting to teach how to "read" the postures and actions of others for what they "really mean." People can begin to believe they know what someone else is thinking, particularly someone close to them. This kind of mind reading often leads to false conclusions, however, and a kind of paranoia can develop. A paranoid person is, in fact, a good example of mind reading taken to an extreme. People who exhibit features of paranoia seldom check out their thoughts, since they are convinced they know the truth and others would only lie to cover it up.

Another variation of mind reading is personalizing the random actions of others. For instance, from time to time I respond in anger or frustration when I hear a horn honk while I am on the freeway. I act as though it is directed at me personally, even though there are many other cars on the road toward which the honk might be directed. In fact, it might even be a friendly greeting rather than an unwelcome criticism. By distorting my thoughts in this manner, however, I can be in a very foul mood by the time I arrive at work. Deciding "it's going to be one of those days" usually follows a set of random events that one personalizes in this very same manner. It also leads one to look for even more ways in which he might be slighted during the day.

Some people become so sure they can read minds and that others want to hurt them that they jump to conclusions. They make big decisions with little information, interpreting all sorts of things from a glance, an absence, or just a few words. This is particularly destructive to intimate relationships. Arguments often begin because one party misunderstands or reads into what the other is saying without checking it out. Depressed people are very vulnerable to this type of error. Like horses with black blinders on, they see only a narrow range of life and consistently interpret the actions and words of others in the worst possible way. Some have tried to justify this kind of outlook with cynicism, saying that it helps them avoid being disappointed, but who could be more disappointed than one who expects the worst from everyone?

Janet, an attractive woman being treated for depression, described this scenario: "I was in the kitchen rushing to get dinner ready when my husband came in. He didn't even say 'hi' before he asked me to go jogging with him tonight. I know he was trying to make me feel guilty because I'm fat."

Janet's tendency to read other people's minds and jump to conclusions was not limited to reactions toward her husband. She was often upset and depressed because of her assumptions about what other people said or did. She accepted a challenge to check out her assumptions before they made her miserable, beginning with her husband. When he invited her to go jogging again, she discovered he really just wanted someone to run with; he was not necessarily critical of her weight. Taking a moment to check out her conclusions made a big difference in her thoughts, and therefore, in her feelings also.

The remedy for mind reading and jumping to conclusions is simple yet very difficult for some: check it out. Asking for more information or sharing your interpretation will give people a chance to accept or reject your conclusion.

Another form of omniscience is the belief we can foretell the future, and to depressed people, it usually looks bleak. By expecting sorrow and pain, they seem to hold a sieve that catches whatever is negative or hurtful and allows other experiences to pass through. Positive experiences are especially likely to be filtered out instead of being enjoyed or savored. Disappointments are retained and become overwhelming. A depressed person might say, "How can I enjoy anything when I'm so fat?" or "After he said I had let him down, it ruined my whole day" or "I just couldn't face them again, I felt so embarrassed."

Because of the person's inability to focus on what is good or constructive, potential positives can be twisted into negatives. We presume that we know better than to accept that something good is happening. Joan, for example, passively looked for work off and on for several years. If any job began to look promising, however, she came up with a number of objections to it. When she received the highest score on a test for one job and was told she would be contacted in a few days, she immediately began to generate reasons why the job would be unsuitable for her. She even mentioned the number of bumps on the road leading to the office building where she would work. To hear her talk, the job offer was not to be celebrated—it was almost catastrophic.

Depressed people also frequently ignore or deny any compliments or recognition they are given because it is inconsistent with their gloomy picture of themselves. A common thought is, "If he knew what I was really like, he wouldn't say that." Of course no one will ever know everything about someone else, and even if they could, chances are they would not judge us as harshly as we fear. Absolute perfection is not required to receive or enjoy a compliment anyway. When we refuse to accept positive strokes from people, they usually stop coming our way, since few people are willing to argue with someone over whether they look nice or did a good job. Depression decreases the ability to feel good about what someone says; yet it increases sensitivity to any negative feedback. Looking for and accepting the positive can bring us back into balance. Even just acknowledging compliments keeps them coming rather than closing the door, and it doesn't frustrate the one who gives the compliment.

One girl in my high school class was so good at negating compliments that almost everyone gave up on her. She flatly refused to accept that anything was positive, and she seldom smiled. For a while we thought Pat was just sad about something, and we continued to try to cheer her up. After a few months, however, her gloominess began to affect others profoundly. We felt powerless and stopped inviting her along. In retrospect, I can see that Pat's negative attitude prevented us from reaching her. She filtered out all our attempts to cheer her, and we felt put down and ineffectual. At our ten-year reunion I saw Pat again. She had not changed much, even though she now had a new group of associates and some years had passed. I realized again that the change had to come from within her. Perhaps she will wait her whole life for someone or something to make the difference that only she can make.

Pat, like other depressed people, could benefit from focusing on positives, even looking actively for them, and accepting the support, compliments, and caring of others. This is a real struggle when we're feeling down, because it is more natural to dwell on the negative. Filters seem to fall over our eyes. Just as polarized glasses keep out glare, so depressing thoughts keep us from experiencing the joyful and positive; we can see only the negative or hurtful. If we remove these filters, even try some "rose-colored glasses," our mood improves.

Depressed individuals become overly sensitive to the actions, words, and even thoughts of others. They believe that everyone is watching them and reacting critically. This belief can lead to self-consciousness and an inability to properly perceive their influence or importance to others. Often individuals will avoid making decisions or taking action because they fear what people will think of them. While we may seem to be in a powerful position when we believe that what we do is of so much interest, it is usually a false belief. Actually, the most devastating thing about what other people think about us is to realize they rarely do. We need to move away from the center of the universe and be content to just be ourselves. Developing a realistic perspective is a challenge when we are depressed, but it is essential to improving our mood.

Shoulds

"I really should try the suggestions in this book, but . . . " Whenever I hear someone say "should," I assume the person won't. *Shoulds* are usually a way to acknowledge some desire or obligation and then dismiss it.

Think of the number of times you use the word *should*. How may *shoulds* do you actually follow through with? *Shoulds* often become ammunition for self-persecution and destruction of self-image rather than assets. At this moment I can think of ten or twelve things I should (and could) be doing, but I *am* writing this chapter. I have to decide for myself what is most important and fit in other activities as I can. If I feel guilty because of my choices, I am likely to not enjoy what I am doing and to resent those activities I *should* be engaged in. No study that I am aware of indicates that guilt or resentment leads to positive growth and change.

Think of a busy time recently when you had what seemed like a million things to do, maybe a holiday, a special party, or vacation preparation. Most people experience increased stress, even when they are happy about an important upcoming event. It is common to feel overwhelmed, lose the ability to concentrate, become cranky, and wish it was just over with. *Shoulds, musts,* and *oughts* give us stress in this way too. They are those millions of things that probably won't get done but take energy to worry about: the untidy attic, the letter to an old college pal, the scrapbook that needs to be arranged, and the thank-you notes to the folks who helped with the ward party. They are the gnawing pit in our stomach when we think of what we *should* do today and the beginnings of an overly guilty conscience.

A serious mistake is made by assuming that *shoulds, musts,* and *oughts* are really our conscience or the Holy Ghost attempting to direct us. These spiritual feelings do occur, and we can strive to accurately recognize their source by staying in tune. Usually, however, *shoulds* are leftovers, the rules or expectations of someone we have wanted to please.

Resentment of *shoulds* is also a major cause of guilty feelings. Trying to please everyone and fulfill all of our *shoulds* generates frustration. For example, we think we *should* keep an immaculate home as our mother did, but she didn't work outside the home as well. We *should* play football as our brother did. We *should* enjoy each and every church meeting, and if we don't, something is wrong with us. *Shoulds* can become a heavy burden, sometimes more than we can bear.

A handsome young man became depressed and somewhat of a recluse. He thought that whatever he did *should* have been done better, or he *should* have done something else. He was immobilized by his many self-critical *shoulds*, avoided attempting almost anything in order to escape this criticism, and, consequently, found little satisfaction in life. He was also constantly disappointed in people because he extended his unrealistic expectations to them. Those who might have been friendly avoided his rigid demands and judgment.

Directing *shoulds* toward our family and friends is likely to damage our relationships. A response we think should occur may not be natural for someone else. For instance, a newly married couple faced the dilemma of what they *should* do when one of them was sad. The husband thought people should be left alone to lick their wounds (that's what he wanted). His wife, however, thought people should try to provide comfort (that's what she wanted). Disappointment and confusion occurred until they each let go of their *shoulds* and responded instead in a manner that pleased their partner.

This is a very common pattern. *Shoulds, musts,* and *oughts* seldom stay inside us. They are like a communicable illness, creeping onto our friends and acquaintances. If these thoughts get out of control, they can destroy our own self-esteem and our relationships with others.

Letting go of *shoulds* can be accomplished in a variety of ways. For example, try using *won't* or *will* instead of *should, ought,* or *must.* You will be making a clearer statement of your intentions and reassume control over your decisions. A less radical and more ambiguous word is *may.* This puts you back in charge. It lets people know that you haven't decided yet. When a *should* appears, identify whom it really belongs to. Is it your mother's? your ex-bishop's? your brother's? Give it back to them; tell yourself, "I know you wanted me to do this, but it does not fit for me."

A recent popular book was titled *Pulling Your Own Strings.* Banishing *shoulds* will cut some of the strings from others that tie us to depression, and it will allow others to pull their own strings too.

Extremes

Life can feel like an emotional roller coaster with unpredictable changes in mood. Depressed people commonly feel this way because they think in extremes of highs and lows. Remember the wise and foolish men who built their houses on different foundations. The wise man built his house on rock; the foolish man built his on sand. (See Matthew 7:24-27.) Emotional homes are too often built on the shifting sand of feelings rather than the rock of reality. Being out of touch with the world around us leads to distortion and depression.

An example of extreme thinking is the use of absolute language that defines the world as black or white, all or nothing, leaving little room for uncertainty or partial satisfaction. Can you think of something that is absolute? A totally clean house, a perfect lesson, and an absolute disaster are all exaggerations; they exist only in our minds.

The real world is not made up of absolutes, but of mixtures. A few pure elements have been combined to create a rich variety of life on earth. So it is with mortal life. Absolute good and bad are hard to find; most experiences are some kind of combination. Even physicists are learning that their old rules of how the world *had* to operate must bend or change to encompass what they are now learning. When we use words like *never, always, all,* or *none,* we pretend that the world is made up only of opposites or absolutes. People who say they are *always* wrong or *never* on time or their work is appreciated by *no one*, for example, are just plain wrong. If they begin to believe these ideas, they may stop trying to improve themselves. Thoughts like these cause disappointment and the anticipation of disappointment because they lead a person to assume he will fail.

A woman who had recently returned from a vacation described her trip as a "total disaster." Her companions were insensitive, they had been "conned" at the airport, and the weather was too hot. She mentioned only in passing making new friends, broadening her horizons by traveling (she had not previously traveled outside her home state), and how inspired she felt when she saw some of our national treasures. It was clear that she had become depressed because of her negative focus and outlook. The report of her travels sounded depressing because of her exaggerations.

Sometimes it requires intense concentration to find a positive thought, but it is a skill we can learn. Start by ridding yourself of absolutes, the major contributor to extreme thinking. Words like *always, never, everyone,* and *nobody* are a red flag. When you think or say these words, stop and ask yourself, "Am I exaggerating?" Depressed people frequently think and speak in absolutes, and in this way they keep their world simple and simply awful.

Depressed individuals may also swing to the other extreme and minimize or underestimate the real importance of some things. Depression increases vulnerability to temptations; self-image becomes so low that ideals that were once important don't seem to matter any more.

A young man struggling with depression had recently returned to school, fulfilling one of his important goals. He had been looking forward to a fresh start. When he became mildly depressed, however, he began to skip classes and not complete assignments, minimizing the impact of these decisions by telling himself each night that tomorrow he would catch up. Soon he was overwhelmed with catch-up work. His perspective was changed by depression, and the dream of college became a nightmare.

Many couples I have seen in therapy have also developed serious problems when they have minimized the importance of their relationship or their partner's needs. It is common that at least one member of a couple seeking marital therapy is also suffering from depression; minimization, which often accompanies it, can be one of the causes of marital problems.

Another common error of extremes is to take a little information and draw a broad conclusion from it. Imagine a child taking her first wobbly step, falling down, and concluding "I'll never walk." Some of us are lucky we learned what we did when we were young! Jumping to extreme conclusions causes us to avoid many potentially pleasurable activities. The ability and motivation to attempt something new decreases when we adopt a pessimistic attitude and growth is stunted. Depression can result because we feel that we are stuck in a rut.

Depressed people frequently think that problems are outside of their control and believe there is nothing they can do to change them. This extreme conclusion usually causes them to give up. We all have experiences that are out of our control at times, but it is an error to predict, because of these events, that our actions never make a difference. Some have speculated that feeling a lack of control in life over a period of time can stimulate a form of depression called "learned helplessness." Passivity often results, even in a situation where action may make a difference, because the individual thinks he has no power to control or change things; he has, in effect, learned to respond in a helpless manner. Such persons attribute the ability to avoid negative situations to luck or chance. The belief that they are stuck in a rut becomes inviolable, even when they could improve the situation by taking some action.

For example, every winter Fred was depressed from

mid-November to mid-January. It seemed to have always been that way for him. He had grown up in a large family where money was scarce and the holidays were celebrated austerely. As a boy he compared his Christmas gifts with those of his friends, and he felt disappointed. As an adult he fantasized that his friends would initiate contact with him to cheer him up, but they did not meet his expectations. Each year he gave in to depression and acted as though he were powerless to alter this pattern. Though he could have organized pleasant activities on his own, he chose to remain passive and to feel hopeless. He thought, "It's no use. I'll just have to get through it one more year."

Fred had developed a type of learned helplessness through a long series of disappointments around Christmastime. He really could not do much about his family's lack of money, and perhaps as a youngster he didn't have the skills to organize activities with his friends. For a while he passively accepted his misery as unavoidable each year. Now, however, he actively arranges positive interactions with his friends and family, and he feels much happier during the holidays.

Patience and Practice

Man has long sought a perpetual motion machine, a machine that, once started, would keep going on its own. Depression is like this machine. Initial sadness triggers in us automatic negative thoughts and a lack of interest in usually pleasant activities. We then withdraw from others, put on blinders that filter out positives, and focus on our negative experiences. There is even some evidence that memory for negative experiences is sharpened during periods of depression. This process can be halted if we recognize and change those patterns of thinking and behaving that perpetuate blue moods.

To achieve a greater measure of joy in our lives, we can begin to recognize distorted, destructive thought patterns in ourselves and use some of the specific techniques provided here to change them. These techniques are like tools, however; it takes practice to become expert at using them.

I learned about the importance of patience one Christmas when I wanted to make an intricate piece of furniture and had to use a router. The router had sat unused on the shelf for some years. At first the tool seemed awkward to use, and I made gouges in the wood. I thought it would take forever to complete the project. Then, with practice, I became quite deft and began to enjoy my work. I found I was getting better, so much so that the router almost felt like a natural extension of my hands. The project was completed in time, and I was proud of my work.

Take a moment and decide where to begin your work. Which distortions are most common for you: Labeling; Omniscience, Omnipotence, Overgeneralizing; Shoulds; or Extremes? On an index card that will fit in your pocket or purse, begin writing down examples of your distorted thoughts. Set aside a few minutes each day to review what you have written and think of more rational responses. Enlist the help of family or friends to monitor what you say; perhaps you can make it into a game among you by competing to become the most realistic. Then use the specific ideas presented here with each type of error. Exchange your negative, automatic thoughts for positive or at least neutral ones. Since negative thoughts often become second nature, eliminating them requires practice and hard work. Nevertheless, I am confident you will feel more joy if you work with these tools to control your thoughts, and in doing so, you will improve your feelings.

Chapter 2

CONTROLLING OUR ENVIRONMENT

Some mornings I jump out of bed feeling energized and excited about the day, even if I have not slept much the night before. Sometimes, though, the alarm rings and I can't seem to get up until I am almost late. While I'm frozen in bed, I try to think of a good reason to get up: Is there anything novel about today? Is there any real reason not to get up? Is there anything good to eat if I do get up? When I finally force myself out of bed, I look for little things I *must* do before work—petting the cat, changing clothes again, or anything to stall. These variations in our attitude happen to all of us now and then, and many times the difference between the feelings of excitement and those of depression on these mornings is based on our anticipation of the day's events.

Peter Lewinsohn and his colleagues at the University of Oregon have studied the relationship between depression and the quality of an individual's experience with his environment. They have theorized that a decrease in pleasant events and/or an increase in unpleasant events leads to a change in how rewarding he perceives the world to be. If he is facing a great deal of stress or uncertainty in comparison to positive experiences, for example, the scales may tip in the direction of a blue mood. Not everyone will become depressed when under pressure, however, since each person is unique. An individual's responses also vary depending on the situation, the timing of negative events, and personal resources.

One consistent difference between depressed and non-depressed individuals is their attitudes about control and responsibility for their lives. According to psychiatrist Aaron Beck's theory of learned helplessness, depressed individuals believe that control over most decisions and events in life is out of their hands and is determined instead by decision-makers, such as their boss, their spouse, their bishop, or maybe just fate. This belief contributes to a depressive, downward spiral. An initial sense of hopelessness leads to a decrease in motivation to take charge of life, an increase in feeling out of control, and then the blues. Exercising control over the events of daily life is critical in alleviating depression.

The idea of controlling our environment may sound like science fiction. Images from books such as *Brave New World* and *1984* come to mind and may frighten us a little. Shaping the world in positive and useful ways has proven to be a powerful tool for combatting depression, however, and is already being used on us every day. For example, the last time you purchased groceries there was probably music (or more precisely Muzak) playing throughout the store. Notice it the next time you are shopping. It will not likely be a rousing piece such as "The William Tell Overture" or modern rock and roll, but a soothing, gentle melody designed to make you feel like lingering. Its purpose is to keep you in the store longer and therefore buying more (research has shown that it works, too). Computer manufacturers are also using the magic technique of controlling the environment by creating "user friendly" hardware and software programs. If you make a mistake on this type of computer, it will not display a cold and punishing word like "error," or flash "tilt" while smoke pours out of the keyboard. The computer acts politely and writes "Please try again" or even provides suggestions on how to get it right. One company has put the controls right in your hand so you only have to point at whatever it is you want it to do. Using this kind of technology has paid off handsomely for computer makers. People prefer "user friendly" equipment because it provides a positive environment for working and it helps them feel good. You can program your life like these computers with a daily dose of good, positive experiences.

Feeling in control of one's environment can do wonders for any individual, and a depressed person especially needs to find the ways to regain control. Some general principles of controlling environment are presented here. Choose from among the suggestions those ideas which seem most relevant to your situation, and experiment with changes in your style of interacting with the world around you.

The Little Things

Nina sat quietly in group therapy. She began to feel hopeless and trapped as she thought about going home to her three young children, fixing them dinner, and spending the night alone. Another group member, noticing the despairing look on her face, commented on her silence and sadness. "I don't have anything to look forward to," Nina explained. "Every day is just the same." Members of the group then began to discuss what they each found rewarding in life. The answers were as varied as the personalities of the group members: a hot bath and reading a good magazine or book, taking five minutes to do yoga, making cookies, calling a friend, sleeping in, giving the family bird a bath, and going to the library to get new books. Nina was surprised they could feel joy in such little things. She seemed to be waiting for a grand something to change her life from dull to exciting and to lift her out of depression.

Nina will probably be waiting a long time. Most of us

have a fairly set routine in life. We know what to expect from each day, and may experience few variations in our routine. It is easy to identify with Sisyphus, the mythical king of Corinth, who was condemned by the gods to forever roll a boulder up a hill in Hades, only to have it roll down again as he neared the top. Focusing on the daily grind is not the way to increase pleasure in life, however. Negative thoughts about the tasks of the day can stall progress before we have even started to try; we then languish in bed searching for the energy to get up or perhaps a good excuse not to. When we believe life is made up only of "have-to's," depression is likely to follow.

"Aha," you may say, "I knew it was my job that was getting me down. I've felt like quitting for a long time." Blaming job, family, neighbors, friends, or others for the daily unpleasantness we face is deceptively easy. Placing the responsibility for happiness somewhere else, outside of ourselves, often contributes to thoughts about drastic solutions, such as a job change, a move, or a divorce. In some situations these alternatives might be part of the answer. For most people, though, a few minor changes can bring a lot of joy and satisfaction to life. You might be surprised, as Nina was, at the pleasure to be gained from programming little extras into daily life.

Following group that evening Nina sat down and wrote out a list of the little things that bring her pleasure. The only qualifications for inclusion were that they be within her reach financially and immediately at hand with little advance preparation. Here is her list:

1. Play a game with my oldest son after the other children are asleep.
2. Decorate a cake.
3. Invite a friend over to watch a movie.
4. Walk through the local aviary.
5. Get out my candy molds and make some candy.
6. Drive up into the mountains and get out of the smog.

7. Take a hot bath before I pick up my kids from the baby sitter.

8. Do some crossword puzzles for a few minutes.

9. Rearrange the furniture in my front room.

10. Give my bird a bath.

Nina was pleased with her list. Even thinking about doing something just for fun gave her spirits a lift. The next step was to put her thoughts into action. As she planned out the rest of the week, she made sure one or two of these activities were included each day. Some of them, such as baths and crossword puzzles, she could do often. Others she wouldn't want to do more than once in a while. I encouraged her to hang the list in a place where she could see it often and add to it when she had new ideas. If she felt depressed, choosing something fun from it to do might help improve her mood.

Programming positive and pleasant activities into life is a centerpiece of many behavioral approaches to treating depression. Although many people report experiencing a lack of pleasure in any activity when they are depressed (this is called anhedonia), doing almost anything that is potentially pleasurable seems to help. This is often a difficult concept to grasp because it involves a paradox: doing what one least wants to do and yet gaining an improvement in mood from it.

Good places to start looking for helpful little diversions are memories of what you have enjoyed in the past. Take out a sheet of paper and begin to generate a list. Remember the two rules: the activities have to be financially reasonable and they must be immediately at hand. These are very short-term activities, goals, and projects. Going to Europe or finding a new job are too demanding for this list, but sending a letter for travel information or a class schedule might be appropriate *if* they sound like fun. When you run out of ideas, post the list in a handy place and add to it when you can. Plan to fit one or two of these activities into every day. Don't approach the ideas passively and just hope you can work them in. Make a space in your life. There will be more energy for the "have-to's" if you take time for some "want-to's."

Learning to Set Limits

Kent was a young man in a hurry. He felt far behind his peers because he was nearing thirty and had not completed college, so he decided to return to school. He did not want to decrease his standard of living, so he took on an extra job. He had also become accustomed to a healthy social life and wanted to keep it. After a few weeks of this hectic schedule, Kent became depressed. "It seems like all I do is get up, get dressed, go to school, go to work, come home, and crash," he said. "I never have any fun and I never have time for myself." Kent had forgotten that he had made the choice to try to do everything at once, and now life felt like an unbearable burden.

This situation is not unusual. People often create their own monstrous schedules by wanting to do *everything, all* the time. The cost can be great to our health, our family life, our sense of well-being, and, perhaps, our general feeling of sanity. Many people need to slow down or rearrange the priorities in their lives in order to achieve an improvement in mood.

One of the reasons for this earth life is to learn how to become like God. Genesis states that the work of creation was divided into six days, and on the seventh, there was rest. There are two notable ideas in this description: God did not attempt to do *everything* in one day, and the scriptural emphasis on the eternal principle of taking time to rest and reflect. Let's examine both ideas more closely.

For whatever reason, the world, like Rome, was not created in a day. We do not know why the creative period was divided instead of completed all at once. It would be reasonable to assume, however, that the Creators worked in accordance with eternal laws and principles as the earth was being formed. As mere mortals, in comparison we would be wise to consider ourselves as subject to some practical limitations too.

An important place to begin setting limits is to avoid not overwhelming ourselves with too many demands, regardless of how worthwhile the cause might be. Barbara, an active Latter-day Saint, said that she had been taught to "pull till you drop, like the pioneers and their animals did." She related a story about a pioneer woman who had been run over by a wagon, breaking both of her legs. Because others in the company could not care for her and were under pressure to move on, they shot her. While I doubted the accuracy of the story, its impact on Barbara was clear. For her, the journey through life is a burden to be borne and your worth is determined by how much you can bear. She thought that the idea of setting limits or organizing positive and enjoyable activities for yourself was tantamount to sin. It was not surprising that she had felt blue and overwhelmed for years!

Balancing Work and Rest

The second principle illustrated by the story of the Creation in Genesis is achieving a balance between work and rest. The work of creation was followed by a period of rest and renewal. Medical research is rapidly establishing the dangers of a workaholic lifestyle: increased risk of heart attacks, strokes, high blood pressure, and any other stress-related illness. Doubtless most people who drive themselves to these extremes believe it is necessary to suffer in order to succeed. Whatever project they are working on becomes more important than anything else, and they fail to respect the natural limitations of their body and spirit. Eventually the body will get their attention through disease and illness, and the spirit may demand consideration by losing energy and initiative (something we have learned to call depression).

Even when the goals being pursued are of unquestionable importance, there are limits to what one can do, as Kent learned while fulfilling his dream of returning to school. Though his time was committed to worthwhile tasks, he had previously derived much satisfaction from planning spur-of-the-moment activities with his friends and taking time off to relax by himself occasionally. He lost the flexibility he once had to be spontaneous and began to feel as if his life was being controlled by someone else. He rebelled (against himself, perhaps), cut classes, put off homework, and called in sick to work. He was trying to feel free again, but was saddled by increasing depression instead.

When Kent came in for therapy, he was desperate; his dream had turned into a nightmare. At first he resisted the idea of slowing down by making a lot of "should" statements, such as, "I should be able to do all this" and "I should be happy just to be back in school—it's what I've always wanted." Then he seemed to realize that joy isn't found in the way things *should* be, but in the way they really *are*. He decided to cut back the number of classes he was taking, to work one night less a week, and to spend less money on entertainment to make up the difference. In the following weeks his enjoyment of life increased dramatically. The former chores became pleasures, and he savored his positive feelings from being back in school. His experience taught him that there really can be too much of a good thing. By taking on more than we can do, we may end up not enjoying any of it or even resenting our involvement.

The principle of rest is presented along with creation in scripture. God has wisely commanded man to rest and worship Him on the Sabbath, but the importance of rest extends beyond Sunday, as does that of worship. This principle of rest is not understood by many people. Rest is mistakenly confused with sleep, which is only one of many forms it may take. The quality that makes sleep restful is its potential to recharge or invigorate our bodies and minds when we are tired.

Recreational activities can be (but are not always) restful. Some people respond with anxiety to highly competitive or challenging activities. The key concept of rest is rejuvenation, literally a re-creation of energy in life. Often people are unaware of how to rest and re-create. For instance, though we may engage in several sports activities, these might not provide the kind of diversion that is needed. We all have to discover what is really restful for *us*, and the discovery for each of us is likely to be different. It is similar to our personal tastes in food; what is a delight to you may be difficult for me to swallow.

To identify what is restful to you, think about the last time you really felt at ease and at peace. What were you doing? Reading a book by the fireplace? Taking a leisurely evening walk? Having a quiet dinner with a friend? Singing along with a record? Everyone is going to have a different answer, and your own choices of restful activities will change with your mood and circumstances, too. Develop a list of potential ways to rest that you can choose from when you're out of ideas. Take time to rest. You need and deserve it.

Handling the "Have-to's"

Sometimes we have to do things that are unpleasant, such as spring cleaning, talking to a creditor, or writing a lengthy report. These things are all part of life, and they cannot be ignored. What can be done is to use creativity in organizing these tasks in ways that will minimize our personal stress. Here are a few suggestions:

1. *Be a Tom Sawyer.* Remember when Tom was forced to whitewash the fence? Instead of doing it all by himself, a most unpleasant task, he enlisted the help of others—and they even paid him for the privilege. Not everyone has Tom's skills at selling others on the joy of tedious projects, but we can often make a task easier by getting more folks involved. Family and friends are natural allies to call on when there is a need (we would, of course, be available to help them with something later). Frontier communities had this kind of tradition; they combined forces for "house raising," and by helping

each other, they could accomplish much more than if they worked individually. Don't overlook co-workers on the job or in the Church as other possible sources of help.

2. *Try not to take on too many disagreeable tasks at once.* The sheer multitude of them can get you down. Learn to recognize when something is difficult for you, and say no if you already have a backlog of unpleasantries. Since unpleasant tasks are usually the easiest to procrastinate, you court crisis and depression by tackling several disagreeable jobs at once. Schedule them in a few at a time or a piece at a time.

3. *Reward yourself after you've worked on a "have-to."* These rewards can be very simple and still be effective, such as a light snack, a phone call to a friend, or an evening walk. When I was a boy, my dentist would let me choose a plastic ring or other trinket from a case after he had filled my teeth. My last memory of him was positive, and it seemed to relieve some of the previous pain. Positive reinforcement can be used by adults, too, and help us feel more like tackling the tough jobs in the future.

Learning to Say No

One of the most important strategies to assist us in arranging our life in a positive and rewarding manner is to learn when to say no. Of course, everyone can make those sounds with his mouth; the skill comes in knowing when and how to say it. For instance, I have been programmed since I was a boy not to say no to requests made of me unless they would clearly be harmful. Before he died, my father left some specific advice about saying no, which was often repeated in my family. "Never say no to a church call." So when I say no, I feel guilty, and if saying yes to a church calling means saying no to myself, I feel angry that I can't have what I want. When I say yes to too many things, I can get depressed.

Several years ago, when I was still in graduate school, I learned an important lesson about saying no and my own mental health. One evening I received a phone call asking me to direct a ward roadshow. I had directed the show the year before, so I was not naive to the many hours and psychological strain involved. At school that quarter I was taking twelve graduate hours (three of them in statistics, which had always been my Waterloo). I was also working two jobs, amounting to above forty hours a week, and was the quorum instructor for the priests in my ward. My first inclination was to decline. Then I remembered what my father had said. "Somehow," I thought, "I'll be able to do all of this." I remembered that when I had directed the roadshow the year before, a minor miracle had taken place when I had received a C in another statistics course (because of my father's injunction, of course).

This was not to be a year of miracles. School was tough and statistics boggled my mind. The roadshow took even more time than the year before. I was racing every minute and felt I wasn't doing well at anything. Depression set in. I felt trapped and unhappy. Had I taken on too much? That would mean I had poor judgment or maybe I just wasn't good enough anymore. Not much solace in those thoughts. I knew something had to give, and my schooling affected only me. I dropped statistics because I had no time to study. The show went on, but my heart wasn't in it. Dropping statistics kept me in school a couple of quarters longer, since it was only offered once a year. Every person to whom I had made commitments paid a price that spring—the cast of the show, my employers, my family, my friends, and me.

How was I to know that directing the roadshow would be too much for me? The truth is, it is probably impossible to always know what our limits are, but there are some things we can do and can watch for.

First—and perhaps most important—we can pray for guidance in deciding whether or not to accept a new opportunity. Each of us is entitled to receive personal revelation for our own life, and we need to tap this spiritual source whenever we have a difficult decision to make.

Second, if we are already overwhelmed, we should seriously consider whether one more demand can be met. Sometimes when people are under stress, a new opportunity looks particularly appealing, like a chance to break out of the grind. Perhaps there is really an option to do some schedule juggling, delay something else, or leave another project undone while fitting something else in, but we need to be careful. People are most vulnerable to bad decision making when they're overtaxed. We might be running away from current pressures instead of making a positive change.

Third, we need to think about how and where the new request fits in with current priorities and commitments. Some opportunities will eclipse in importance what we are doing right now, and we will want to try and make room for them. Others will be nice offers but not necessary, and if the time and energy are not really there, the new tasks can become like a millstone around our necks, sapping effort that could better be applied elsewhere. Remember, each person is given only twenty-four hours in a day. If we are already pushing our limits, it is doubtful that one more demand on our time will be helpful.

Some people try to avoid setting limits by letting another person decide for them what their limits should be. At times this can lead to serious resentment and rebellion. Frances, who had recently been reactivated in the Church, described her frustration: "I want to go to the temple a couple of times a week; I'm volunteering twice a week at the Genealogical Library and staying after to work on my own research; I've been very busy with the stake welfare project; and now the bishop has asked me to take another call." She felt that one more responsibility would change her enthusiasm into resentment. I encouraged Frances to speak frankly to the bishop about her concerns, and he suggested that she trade the welfare assignment for the new call.

Frances had learned that an important part of her stewardship was to live within her spiritual means. It is a mistake to expect any leader to know exactly what's right for us, particularly when we don't talk to them about the limits we are feeling. Leaders have been appointed to counsel and suggest, not to command in all things. Each one of us must take responsibility for deciding how to spend our time.

When we are altering our environment to correct potentially negative or depressing conditions, a little effort really can make a significant improvement. Often this involves a change in personal style, however, and that is difficult for some to follow through on. Initially, it is a daily effort to redirect our life in a more positive and useful manner, but with perseverance it becomes as natural as an old habit. Making these efforts now will lead to more joy from life in the future.

Chapter 3

DEVELOPING RELATIONSHIPS

Since creation, the link between relationships with others and joy and fulfillment in our lives has been evident. Eve was joined with Adam to be a "helpmeet" or a companion to him, and they were instructed to bear children and find joy in their posterity. Jesus called twelve men to share intimately in his ministry; he had other close relationships as well, such as those with Mary, Martha, and Lazarus. Joseph Smith first shared his vision in the grove with his family; later, many faithful friends cared for him through the trials and hardships of his life. Relationships are important to all of us, regardless of our station in life. We can create joy by strengthening and extending our circle of loved ones.

Each person is born into a unique family. Some are blessed to have a loving mother, father, brothers, and sisters and to grow up knowing how good it feels to be close and to share love. Many people do not have all of these advantages, however. The number of children being raised in families with two parents has been declining steadily for some time. Lifestyles have changed too. Most people do not grow up in the same communities their parents did. Because families move more frequently, children do not have the benefits of grandmothers, grandfathers, aunts, uncles, and cousins living in close proximity as an extended family. Many of us grow up feeling inadequate or unable to relate to others because we have not had the chance to learn the skills of developing lasting relationships.

Sharon was an attractive woman in her mid-twenties, but she stayed at home most of the time and found it hard to relate to people. Most of her friends had taken the initiative to develop a relationship with her. Her parents were also socially isolated. Her father, a workaholic, had little time for others, including his family, and her mother kept to herself. The only relatives of the family lived in distant states, and visits with them were sporadic. Sharon had not learned how to enjoy people or create new friendships, and she feared feeling embarrassed or rejected. For her, relationships were a mystery. She believed it was impossible to learn *how* to make friends; you either knew how or you didn't. Sharon isolated herself, always spoke solemnly and softly, and avoided smiling because she thought her smile was unattractive.

Sharon's story is not unusual. It can be tough to reach outside of oneself to get acquainted with others, particularly during times of depression when one feels inadequate anyway. When I was in junior high school, I sent away for a book titled *Where to Meet Girls and How to Talk to Them,* anticipating that it would contain the secrets of Casanova (or at least the Fonz) and change me from resistible to irresistible. One day a thin envelope arrived, and in dismay I read such "secrets" as these: go to dances or activities at school, church, or clubs, smile, and compliment girls on almost anything. I felt angry to have been taken in by this ploy to rob naive adolescents. However, in retrospect, I can see that the advice was quite sound.

People often believe, as I did about meeting girls, that answers must be complex and mysterious. Americans spend billions of dollars on diet books, pills, foods,

and paraphernalia, but the best and most effective remedy for being overweight still seems to be eat less and
exercise more. I wanted a shortcut to popularity with
minimal effort. Though the advice I received was fairly
simple, I resisted. It seemed backward to push myself to
initiate interaction when I already felt shy and insecure.
I wanted to learn to swim without getting wet.

Depression's Effects on Those Around Us

Do you know someone who consistently seems cheer-
ful, who has a warm greeting and a good word for everyone? You may also know people who are cheerless, unhappy, and cynical whenever you interact with them.
Whom would you rather be with? It has been said, "Misery
loves company." Research indicates, however, that the
miserable are often shunned by others. When we are already depressed, this contributes to increasing depression because we feel rejected. Pat, my depressed high
school classmate introduced in chapter 1, is a good example of this kind of self-perpetuated rejection. Her
constant blues kept others distant from her because they
did not want to be dragged down by her. Our depression
does affect others around us.

College students participating in one research project spoke with depressed and nondepressed individuals
by phone. The students rated the depressed callers more
negatively, said they also felt depressed after making the
call, and were less likely to desire further interactions
with those individuals. In groups, depressed individuals
typically get involved with only a few others, and many
of their interactions are negative, such as complaints,
criticism, or demeaning comments about themselves.
They are also more passive, apparently waiting for
someone else to take the initiative.

Perhaps you can see the paradox. When we are depressed and want to feel close to someone, we are likely
to act in a way that creates distance instead. When we are
self-focused, it is difficult to lose ourselves in others as we

must to create relationships. People typically choose friends and partners who lift them and avoid those who could drag them down; thus, if we have a negative self-image or believe we are only second-rate, we tend to be shunned.

Dependency and Depression

Though relationships are helpful in creating joy and maintaining a positive outlook, it is important to keep them in perspective. There are natural currents, not unlike the tides of the ocean, in most relationships: with our spouse, our friends, or our family. It is normal to feel intense at times and comfortable with some distance at other times. But if we become dependent on love and believe we are nothing without the constant approval and adoration of someone else, we become vulnerable to their excessive or unrighteous demands. I have seen many patients who have developed this kind of dependency, allowing themselves to be abused physically, emotionally, and in some cases spiritually. The beauty of love that they sought became a tragedy in their lives.

The potential hazards of dependency are clearly seen in the desperation that occurs in some people when the intensity of a relationship appears to decline or when one is in between relationships. In these cases, almost any new acquaintance becomes the answer to one's prayers and a way to fill the unfillable void that dependency creates. The new friend frequently feels overwhelmed by this neediness and backs away because he cannot, or does not wish to, fulfill all these unrealistic needs for love and companionship. A handsome, recently returned missionary explained it this way: "If they start to cling to you and you feel like they want to get really serious after only a few dates, watch out!" He stops dating young women who act in this manner even if he likes them and enjoys their company, because they often become jealous and demanding.

Good relationships, contrary to popular myths and

songs on the radio, involve sharing rather than neediness. They frequently flower when two people first feel good enough about themselves to want to give to others. In a recent magazine survey, both men and women were asked what made other people attractive to them, and not one person included any form of neediness in his or her response. By refusing to be needy, and cultivating an open, giving, and friendly persona instead, you will draw others to you.

Intimacy

The word *intimacy* is misunderstood and misused by many people. It does not connote sexuality; indeed, it most often exists without sexual expression. In the three definitions of intimacy in *Webster's New World Dictionary,* sex is never even mentioned, but such words as *private, personal, close, familiar, deep,* and *thorough* are used. Though we often think of love as having a limited quantity, one is capable of being intimate with several people at a time. Like the widow's flask of oil blessed by Elijah because of the widow's willingness to share, love is limitless if used righteously.

Intimate relationships with friends are often ignored as reservoirs of strength. Some people feel they must surrender the right to be close to others when they are married, but this often leads to marital dissatisfaction as one mate struggles to meet needs previously filled by four or five friends. The couple become angry and disappointed in each other because of their unrealistic expectations. This kind of naive togetherness is like putting all your eggs in one basket. Being human, we are bound to trip occasionally in our walk through life. If we can draw strength from others, besides our partners, we are less likely to become depressed during the natural ebbs or trouble spots in that primary relationship.

Some people resist the idea that intimate (and even superficial) relationships require work. Many have been duped into believing the great Hollywood lie that "it just happens." Waiting for the "right" people to fall into our life is a tragic mistake. It is rare to find a person to whom we are drawn from our very first meeting (I can think of two or three in my whole life, and none of them turned out to be my closest friends). In the natural process of friendships, people grow closer together over time in irregular spurts and pauses. True and lasting intimacy requires daring, sharing, and caring over long periods of time. Even if you are lucky enough to fall into a "magic" relationship, you will need to develop new tricks along the way to keep the show going.

The Dangers in Perfectionism

The search for perfectionism is a serious handicap when we are trying to form intimate relationships. Looking at the Washington Monument from a distance, it looks like a smooth, pure-white obelisk; as one gets closer, however, the different colors of stone and effects of aging appear. Often the closer we come, the more faults appear; and for someone looking for perfection, this is very unsettling. Some people avoid getting intimately involved because they cannot find the elusive perfection they seek, and their life and love are wasted on a futile and disappointing search. Looking for perfection can also distance us from others, who back away when they sense our unrealistic expectations.

Perfectionists who are willing to begin a relationship unrealistically idealize their partners to fit their "perfect" image and therefore suffer extreme disappointment and depression when they inevitably must face the fact that their loved one is only human.

David had known Beth only a few weeks, but he was sure she was the girl for him. He thought she was prettier, brighter, and more easygoing than anyone he had ever met. Even though some of his friends told him he was moving too fast, he ignored them and carried himself away in the fantasy he created. David's relationship with Beth continued for about two years. During that time they dated only occasionally, though they saw each other at work a couple of times a week. David's friends and family could not understand his strong attachment to a woman he saw so infrequently, but his lack of contact with Beth did not seem to matter to him. He really worshipped her; she was so right in every way that he sometimes thought that she was too good for him. He began to depend on her love and approval to measure his own self-worth, and he became angry or defensive if anyone suggested that Beth was less than perfect.

One day Beth told David that she wanted to date other men. A week later she told him she was serious about another man and wanted to date him exclusively. David was crushed and angry. She was right for him, and he believed he couldn't find anyone else as perfect. His own self-esteem suffered because he had depended on her love to define his worth as an individual. He became depressed and thought about suicide because he felt he had no more reasons to live; he had put everything into their relationship and their future. Only by confronting the realities about Beth and their uncertain relationship was he able to escape depression, rebuild his self-esteem, and go on with his life.

Though it is romantic to believe that your partner is the answer to all of your dreams, there is danger to you and to the relationship in this fantasy when you finally wake up, as David did. Deification of someone else inevitably brings disappointment. Be content to let others—and yourself—be human and fallible. Try to love people for what they are rather than what you wish them to be, and both you and they will find greater happiness in being together.

Growth Through Others

Relating to someone in a positive and growth-promoting manner helps us to progress toward godhood and can help diminish our chances of experiencing serious depression. God's work and glory are to bring about the immortality and eternal life of men. Is there a greater work for us than to join in this effort by developing relationships that are mutually uplifting? According to Abraham, God recognized the need for growth and progression among the intelligences that surrounded Him. He organized spirits and later bodies for them because of His love and the glory they would bring to Him. (See Abraham 3, 4.) We also can assist those around us in reaching their full potential and, thereby, expand ourselves.

Seek relationships in which both parties can win. Too often individuals compete instead of complementing each other. Friendships that have an underlying competitive base seldom stand up over a long period of time or achieve a level of commitment that allows real growth. Imagine friendship as a three-legged race; one person cannot win without the other.

Consider what impact your current set of friends has on you. Adults often look at teenagers in dismay as previously "good" kids fall in with the "wrong" crowd and begin to imitate the bad habits of their peers. We fool ourselves if we believe this phenomenon is limited to teens, however. Older "birds of a feather" also flock together, and one would be wise not to nest among the looney birds! Luckily, the company we keep can also encourage, challenge, and strengthen us. Don't be afraid to walk away from negative interactions or relationships and to seek friends among positive, vibrant people who will lift you.

Developing Relationships

Here are a few simple but effective suggestions for making interactions with other people more pleasant and more likely to develop into growthful relationships. As you experiment with them, you will find others responding more positively and more frequently to you.

1. *Smile.* Smiling is the universal symbol of friendliness; it is a signal that you are approachable and

friendly. Advertisers know that smiles sell products; why not put this technique to work for you too? Practice smiling more frequently for a week or two. If you are reluctant to smile at strangers, start with your family or close friends. Ask them to help you remember to smile. Think about funny stories or jokes you have heard or imagine ridiculous situations, such as a dog wearing a business suit or other absurdities, if you need promptings in order to smile. Your smile will draw people toward you; it will break through barriers between you and other people. Perhaps, best of all, you will begin to feel happier too.

2. *Say hello.* When you have mastered smiling (or even before), add a greeting to your smile. Most people enjoy being acknowledged by others, and saying hello gives you the chance to deepen your encounter. Do not be discouraged if not everyone returns your warmth; think of yourself as a "missionary of joy," and understand that not everyone will accept your message. This may seem difficult, particularly if you think of yourself as a shy person, but the rewards are great. A greeting is usually the first step in a conversation.

3. *Focus on the other person.* We all like to feel that we are important, so capitalize on this by taking an interest in others. Ask them about their family, job, hobbies, or opinions, and let them express themselves without being criticized. You will get to know more about them and they will almost certainly feel flattered by your interest. Talk-show hosts are good examples of people who get to know others by encouraging them to talk about their interests. Pretend you are interviewing your new acquaintances; help them to feel comfortable and important, and they will almost certainly enjoy your company. Make a game out of practicing this new social skill, and you'll soon be looking forward to chances to practice instead of dreading meeting others.

4. *Focus on the positive.* People like to be complimented and to hear good things about others too. Cultivate the skill of seeing the good in everyone. This is

a truly Christlike quality that will draw people to you and improve your current relationships. Others will feel comfortable opening up to you because you do not engage in gossip or criticism. Practice saying a positive word or giving a compliment to everyone you meet.

5. *Take the initiative.* Most of us interact every day with people who could become friends if we initiated a few contacts with them. Co-workers, neighbors, classmates, and old acquaintances are just a few examples of people we already know with whom we might form lasting relationships. They are potential sources of new energy for our lives, but it takes some effort to tap these sources. Depressed people tend to be passive, to sit back and say, "If they want to be my friend, they will let me know." Chances are you might feel inadequate or have low self-esteem; you are afraid to take the risk to invite them over or to share lunch with you. Unfortunately, there is no other way to increase your circle of friends. The adage "nothing ventured, nothing gained" is certainly true in relationships. Not everyone we approach will want to become close to us, but we will learn and grow through trying. Just as few people bowl or ski or play tennis with accuracy and finesse the first time, we may need a little practice with the skills of relationship building before we begin to see success.

Take a minute and consider those with whom you might initiate a contact: perhaps a new ward member (they are usually open to meeting friends), someone you frequently sit by in church, or an old high school or college friend. Now think of a way to begin or deepen the relationship: a plate of cookies, a no-occasion card, an invitation to dinner. There are many ways to approach people without feeling overwhelmed or vulnerable; just use your imagination. Though not everyone will become your best friend, they will surely be flattered by your kindness and you will have taken some important steps toward taking control of your interactions with others.

6. *Use and expand your social network.* When we feel

lonely, we often fail to think about what resources there are for meeting others. One therapy group that I led was composed mostly of depressed people who were very lonely, yet they resisted every suggestion to get together outside of group and to offer support to each other. It is easy to overlook possible golden chances to get together with people.

Almost everyone belongs to one or more organizations, such as a church, a business, a hobby club, or a union group. Meetings of these groups are likely occasions to find persons who share at least some of our interests. Take advantage of such encounters to practice some of the techniques described above. Ask people you know for suggestions about how to meet others. Your current friends might even be willing to take you along to a meeting or party where you can mix with another crowd. The Church goes to great lengths to provide opportunities for people of all ages to meet: Primary, Mutual, Relief Society, priesthood, and special interest groups; ward functions, plays, and meetings, and so on. Be brave. Chances are the people you meet are as anxious as you are, but they will admire your courage and be flattered by your attention.

Relationships can provide much needed help on the journey through life, but depending on them in a needy manner is destructive both to ourselves and to those with whom we wish to be close. The proper balance between self-reliance and interdependence must be discovered by each individual based on the unique experience of his or her life.

Chapter 4

PHYSIOLOGY AND DEPRESSION

The early writings of ancient philosophers reflect a debate over the question of the relationship between mind and body. Are they connected? How does one think, experience emotion, and initiate actions? Aristotle (384-322 B.C.) taught that the human heart was the seat of life, motion, and sensation, but he assigned reasoning and thought to the psyche, a portion of each man that was distinct from the body. Today we might recognize the psyche as similar to the modern conception of the soul. St. Augustine (A.D. 354-430) is recognized as the first philosopher to assume that the mind and body are one unit, inseparable from each other. Therefore, whatever affects the mind may affect the body, and vice versa. Though modern science has accepted St. Augustine's notion as fact, many people ignore the intimate connections between how they care for their bodies and how they feel emotionally.

The first task of the psychologist is to rule out potential physical causes for what appear to be psychological illnesses. It is not uncommon for a patient to be referred to a physician before psychotherapy is begun. A medical doctor can properly assess what effect the particular circumstances of an individual's life might have on his mood. A family history of mood disorders, a previous or current physical illness, side effects of any medications, an imbalance in the endocrine system, or metabolic disturbances are all potential culprits in the search for causes of depression. Psychologists recognize the close connection between mind and body; psychological intervention will be futile if underlying physical problems are not controlled. Individuals who have had symptoms of serious depression that have lasted longer than two weeks should therefore consult with a doctor.

Though medication can often help alleviate some of the symptoms of depression, many individuals also require counseling and the initiation of changes in their patterns of thinking and behaving. Depression that has a physical or biological component is often intertwined with a style and pattern of life that must be modified in order for the person to feel well again. Medication alone is not enough to bring about these important changes.

Basic Physical Health

Three basic areas of physical health have an important impact on how we feel from day to day: nutrition, exercise, and sleep. Imbalances in any of these have the potential to compound underlying mood disturbances.

1. *Nutrition.* It has been said that Americans may be some of the most overfed and nutritionally ignorant people on the earth today. Perhaps the saving grace of our overeating is that we are bound to get enough of each major food group, even if it is by chance. Humans literally are what they eat; the building blocks for construction and maintenance of a healthy body must be taken from their daily diet. The essential elements of a balanced diet—carbohydrates, proteins, fats, minerals, and vitamins—are readily available in common foods. Many people have been taught in school that they should eat each day from the four major food categories: milk,

meat, vegetable and fruits, and grains and cereals. A diet that includes these basic and simple elements is enough for almost everyone to stay healthy.

Many sources are available from which we can learn the essentials of nutrition. If a refresher course is needed, a medical self-help book, nutritional pamphlets published by government agencies, workers in the health field, and other resources are readily available. In recent years there has been a surge in the number of books published on nutritional issues. Be careful to avoid faddish diets and books that trumpet undocumented, unrealistic claims about the efficacy of their programs, however. There is no scientific evidence for mega-vitamin therapy or "natural" (health food) cures for depression. Eating sensibly, with a goal of balanced nutrition, is the best regimen for good mental health.

2. *Exercise.* Americans are caught up in a fitness craze, and with any craze come "crazies." Almost everyone who is anyone has written an exercise book or produced a video tape. It is easy to be seduced by the claims of "instant fitness" made by authors or promoters of exercise machines, spa memberships, and other programs. Getting something for nothing appeals to us all. The reality is, however, that time and effort are required before results are achieved. Don't be cajoled into buying anything you will never use just because "it will be good for you." Equipment can be useful only if it is used.

Probably the most important consideration in initiating an exercise program is to do something you enjoy. Few people continue exercising if they don't find some enjoyment in it, and to receive the maximum benefit, exercise must become a regular part of life. It is advisable to consult a doctor before beginning an exercise program and to ask for suggestions about what type of exercise is best for you. Usually, it is wise to begin at a comfortable level and gradually increase your effort. Some people also enjoy exercising with others because of the social contact, mutual support, and encouragement.

3. *Sleep.* The need for sleep is frequently misunderstood and underestimated. Sleep patterns are a good barometer of a person's general well being, and disturbances in sleeping patterns are often indicative of other health problems, especially depression. People who are chronically fatigued are particularly susceptible to illness, may be more inclined to be irritable, are often less able to perform intellectual tasks, and may be less motivated than individuals who have been sleeping well. A recent study of workers who were assigned to rotating shifts indicated they had a much higher incidence of stress-related emotional and physical illnesses than workers performing the same job but on a regular, non-rotating shift. Keeping a regular schedule contributes to one's health.

It is not yet clear why we need to sleep. Some researchers think our brains create toxic substances while we are awake that must be dissipated by sleep. Others believe that dreaming during sleep allows us to consolidate the information accrued during the time we are awake or to develop strategies to deal with current problems we are facing. Whatever the reason, sleep is as much a need as food or water. For the typical person, eight hours of sleep is sufficient, but this varies widely between individuals and for the same person at different times. If you are concerned about the quantity or quality of your sleep, try experimenting with different routines, such as varying your bedtime, the amount of time slept, and the environment in which you sleep, such as the room, the temperature, and the comfort of the bed. Try to maintain some semblance of a regular schedule for sleep after you have discovered the optimal sleeping conditions, too.

Antidepressant Medication

Depression can be a medical problem, and treatment by a physician or psychiatrist may be needed. It is always advisable for everyone to have regular checkups with a doctor; if you are depressed, consulting with a doctor is vital. Depression that has biological causes cannot be resolved by using only nonmedical techniques. Such depression can keep you from feeling as good as you have a right to feel. The number of medical procedures and medications available for diagnosing and treating depression is increasing, and new theories and technology are constantly being developed. Only your physician or psychiatrist can safely use these medical procedures or prescribe medications if they are indicated.

If your doctor decides a medication trial is indicated, you have a right to be informed about any medication prescribed; you will be more likely to follow through with the doctor's recommendations if you understand them.

Some medications are effective in treating depression, though there isn't general agreement about *why* they work. The most widely respected explanation currently is the amine theory, which states that an imbalance exists in chemicals (neurotransmitters) that deliver messages between neurons in areas of the brain that deal with emotion; the antidepressants work to reestablish this natural balance and thus restore more normal moods. A number of medications have been developed that alleviate symptoms of depression in some patients. Most fall into three general families of related drugs: tricyclics, MAO inhibitors, and lithium. Within these families are medications that differ enough in chemical composition that they work better for some individuals than others. Physicians or psychiatrists decide which is best for each patient.

Following is a brief description of each of the three general "families" of antidepressant medications. Since physicians may use the chemical or brand name when talking about medications, both will be included in this listing. The chemical or generic name is given first and some common brand names are included in parentheses.

1. *Tricyclics* are the largest family of antidepressants

and the most commonly prescribed. These include imipramine (Tofranil, Presamine), amitriptyline (Elavil, Endep), desipramine (Pertofrane, Norpramin), nortriptyline (Aventyl), doxepin (Sinequan, Adapin), and protriptyline (Vivactil). It is hypothesized that tricyclics increase the amount of neurotransmitter substance available to carry a message from one neuron to another, and by this action they restore a more normal flow between them.

2. *MAO inhibitors* are prescribed less frequently than the tricyclic antidepressants because of diet restrictions required to prevent potentially serious side effects. They are safe if taken as directed, however. These medications include tranylcypromine (Parnate), isocarboxazid (Marplan), and phenelyzine (Nardil). These drugs probably work by inhibiting other substances that would normally break down transmitter substances, thereby increasing the amount of neurotransmitters available to relay messages between neurons in the brain.

3. *Lithium* is a common salt used to treat a comparatively rare illness, manic depression, which is also referred to as a bi-polar disorder, since one's mood swings from euphoria and much energy to gloom and depression. Even though there are periods of productivity when one is feeling "high," it is a dangerous and potentially life-threatening illness. Individuals who experience these extreme shifts in mood should consult a doctor. The good news about manic depression is how well lithium usually controls the symptoms. Most patients become more productive and happy after beginning the medication procedure because their life levels out and periods of deep depression cease. Other uses for lithium in treating depression are also being explored.

Antidepressant medications have some common features that a doctor can also discuss with you. Here are some of them:

1. These drugs may take about three to four weeks before noticeable changes in depressive symptoms take place.

2. Some patients experience side effects during the first few days they take medications. A dry mouth, drowsiness, constipation, and mild lightheadedness are most common, but they dissipate as the body becomes accustomed to the drug.

3. It is not uncommon for the medication to be changed after several weeks if the doctor does not believe it is as effective as possible. This is not cause for despair, as selecting which medication from which family will work for each patient is an educated guess at best. Researchers are trying to establish criteria for doctors to use in matching patient characteristics with the most favorable medication, but these criteria are not perfected yet.

Some misconceptions and fears about antidepressants exist and should be discussed openly with a doctor. For instance, the notion that using medication to alleviate depression is a sign of personal weakness is an attitude that keeps some people from getting the help they need. Taking an antidepressant is no different from taking insulin for diabetes. In biological depression a physiological imbalance exists that, if untreated, can be dangerous to one's health and well being. Also, being depressed and taking medication for it does not mean one is insane; it is a prudent, wise, and rational choice.

The probability of addiction to these drugs is low. They do not produce reactions of extreme energy and euphoria as do amphetamines, distort reality as do hallucinogens, or have the same sedating qualities as do barbiturates or alcohol. Also, it is not necessary to take increasing amounts to maintain the beneficial effects, as is the case with many other drugs. After a few months the doctor will likely decrease the prescribed dose to a maintenance level or discontinue the medication. If taken as directed by the physician, these medications are safe. Antidepressants do not make moods unnatural or artificial; rather they allow the natural balance and rhythm of life to return.

Chapter 5

THE IMPORTANCE OF SELF-ESTEEM

Much has been written recently about self-esteem. Probably 90 percent of all the people seen for psychological treatment say that they have a low image of themselves, and it doesn't seem to matter if they are attractive or plain, super intelligent or average. Self-esteem is not a mysterious concept, however; it is simply the value *you* place on yourself. You are the judge.

There are many common misconceptions about self-esteem. They lead to ideas like these: "Something must be wrong with me; successful people never feel awkward or experience self-doubt," or "If I just had a better mate, or different friends, a new job, a bigger house, I would feel good about myself," or "If people would say more nice things to me, I would have more self-confidence," or "My parents didn't expect me to amount to much; I'm just a plain person, so no one could really care about me." The basic error underlying all of these misconceptions is the notion that self-esteem is stable, unchangeable, and out of one's control.

Perhaps the most destructive misconception held by many Latter-day Saints is that their self-worth is based on the "sin ratio." In the sin ratio, the number of transgressions is the denominator (the bottom number in a fraction), and the number of good deeds is the numerator (the top number). Since it is usually easier to be in touch with the negative aspects of life or our shortcomings, the denominator is often larger than the numerator, and self-esteem is fractured. We would do well to accept the invitation of the Savior to stop condemning ourselves, and to go our way and disregard our past "sins." (See John 5:14; 8:11.) Jesus understood that focusing on shortcomings and sin is more likely to make us feel hopeless and to destroy our self-esteem than it is to make us feel successful. He did not ignore sin, but He had a balanced view of people as more than just bundles of sin.

Are there good reasons for maintaining a harmful self-image? Of course not, but some people cling to old, negative ways of thinking about themselves as though they were important and beneficial truths. Take a few minutes and make a self-esteem balance sheet for yourself. Write down any advantages you may think of for maintaining a negative image of yourself. Reasons frequently given for keeping a low self-image are: "I won't have to make new efforts to change," "You can't teach an old dog new tricks," and "Other people might think I was conceited if I acted differently." Now list what you might gain by embarking on a program to improve the way you see yourself. Your reasons might include: "I will feel happier and more confident when I meet people," or "I will feel more as if I belong." Compare the two lists and see which one presents the strongest arguments. For most people, in spite of their excuses, it is difficult to make a good case for continuing to feel bad about themselves.

I have sat in countless meetings where children have sung "I Am a Child of God" to an audience of grownups. Invariably as I look about during the singing I see misty- or teary-eyed adults profoundly affected by the message of the song. These same people, however, probably do not often think of themselves as God's children (perhaps they think they have outgrown their heavenly parents?) or treat themselves as potential heavenly kings and queens. They act as if the song is only valid for youngsters, and they seem to have lost their eternal perspective. Adults are more prone to be self-deprecating and self-defeating than self-loving, and their self-esteem pays the price.

Children depend a great deal on parents and other caretakers for sustenance and information about the world. From these messages their first impressions of themselves evolve and become the core of their self-concept. Just as children eventually learn to feed and clothe themselves and provide their own shelter, so do we as adults have the capacity to improve our self-image and develop a new relationship with ourselves. It may not be easy, but it is possible. As adults, we no longer call our parents to find out what to eat for dinner or what to wear to the movie, and we need not be stuck with their opinion of our worth. Not all persons have a bad image of themselves from childhood, of course, nor would this necessarily be the fault of their parents if they did. Still, many people cling to these old, dusty ideas from the past even though they are no longer relevant and certainly not helpful. For instance, even though every chart that lists "ideal" weights indicates I am underweight for my height, I continue to think of myself as fat. My childhood body image (a part of self-image) is clearly not based on current reality.

Labels and Self-esteem

Inaccurate labels are a significant block to good self-esteem. They limit our perspective of who we are and what our real potential is.

A handsome young man with a negative self-concept became depressed when he broke up with a woman he had dated for three years. After a few weeks he thought about going out again, but he felt that he was too shy to attract anyone. He had been shy since his youth, he said, and he expected that he always would be. He believed this label to be as immutable as the color of his eyes. He could not seem to accept the idea that shyness is a way we *act* rather than the way we *are*. The limits prescribed by labels such as shyness are a liability, but they can affect us only as long as we accept them.

Compile a list of labels you have accepted as describing yourself. Do they represent a realistic or a distorted picture? Do they promote confidence and growth, or hesitation and frustration? Share the list with two or three friends or family members, and talk with them about how their perceptions match yours. Invariably people who do this say that their friends are much more positive and less judgmental than they have been. Continuing to indulge in so much self-criticism destroys our self-image. Why not cultivate a more positive attitude?

Self-criticism and Self-esteem

Individuals with low self-esteem frequently spend a lot of time trying to convince everyone else how awful they are. Like Rodney Dangerfield, the comedian, they tell a myriad of stories that could easily begin with "I don't get no respect . . . " They frequently relate tales of woe and misfortune, and self-critical remarks seem to be second nature. These types of behaviors turn off other people; no one who is mentally or emotionally healthy wants to associate with chronic losers. These self-critical individuals often mistakenly believe that if they criticize themselves, they will somehow avoid criticism from others. They cannot, however, provide an example where they avoided a critical remark by using this method; it is probably only as useful as knocking on wood, picking up pennies, and other superstitious acts. Being critical of ourselves actually invites others to focus on our faults.

Self-deprecatory statements are also an ineffective way to avoid appearing conceited or stuck-up. People begin to fear a constantly critical attitude and may think,

"What does he say about me when I'm not around?" If other people accept the self-deprecatory remarks, this strategy to avoid appearing conceited backfires, and legitimate self-pride can be hurt. It is a no-win situation. Self-esteem cannot possibly be improved through self-criticism, and it is up to the individual to change this pattern in his or her life.

Trying to challenge the self-critical attitude of others is difficult, if not impossible. Typically, these individuals discount or ignore positive comments, and we feel less inclined to offer compliments and pleasant conversation in the future. Further, being around people like this makes us feel negated or uneasy. This weakens the self-esteem of everyone involved. Finally, depressed patients who have promulgated this kind of cycle ask in desperation, "Well, what am I good for?" When this point is reached, unfortunately, there is not much good that they will acknowledge, no matter what is said or who says it. Self-esteem has been devastated by chronic self-criticism and refusing the support of others. The best time to work on our self-image is right now, before we reach this kind of crisis. Controlling self-critical remarks is an important first step.

Pride and Self-esteem

Another common symptom of low self-esteem is the inability to enjoy or appreciate one's own accomplishments. Unfortunately, some people confuse pride with boastfulness or conceit. Old sayings such as "Pride goeth before a fall" contribute to this misconception and to wariness about celebrating achievements. Not all pride is conceit, nor is self-pride the opposite of humility, another serious misunderstanding. Though we are counseled to be humble, many individuals are mistaken about what that means. The best example of humility is found in the life and actions of Jesus. He did not deny or condemn His talents, His heritage, or His destiny, nor was He self-deprecatory in any way. He was kind, modest, and unpretentious. He was equally at ease with the poor and the mighty, but constantly aware of His important mission.

Pride can be very healthy. For instance, the recent resurgence of patriotism in the United States has led to new feelings of national pride, as evidenced by the excitement about the 1984 Summer Olympics and efforts to restore such national treasures as the Statue of Liberty. Healthy pride in ourselves and our accomplishments builds a foundation for positive self-esteem and enhances the likelihood that we will do more praiseworthy things in the future. This is a kind of positive reinforcement and recognition that has long been used to increase positive behaviors in children, and it can work just as well with adults. By feeling pride in what we do, we can build ourselves from within, without waiting for others to recognize and acknowledge what we have accomplished.

Rob, a bright young man who had just earned his Ph.D., complained that he felt he had accomplished very little. He shrugged off sincere compliments he received by saying, "It's no big deal. If I could do it, anybody can." He refused to participate in the graduation ceremony or to send announcements to his friends and family. Those close to Rob felt put off by his stoic attitudes and also refrained from celebrating very much, responding to what they thought were his wishes. Rob became demoralized and depressed because he had been waiting for someone else to convince him his doctorate *was* a great accomplishment. He did not realize that this validation had to start from inside himself.

Rob is no different from many of us: from the rich and famous to the poor and lowly, we all want to experience the respect of our peers. We will be disappointed, however, if we wait for the acclaim from without to change our feelings within. Happiness and self-esteem are not always achieved through popular acclaim, as brilliant stars such as Freddie Prinz and Marilyn Monroe have tragically demonstrated by killing themselves at a time when they were admired by millions of people. It is up to us to cultivate and nourish our feelings of self-pride.

The tendency to constantly compare ourselves with others can also contribute to our refusal to take pride in our accomplishments. In comparing, we usually look at only one or two facets of someone's life and decide we are a failure in comparison. This is a faultless path to depression, since it is impossible to be the best at everything. Even if we attained perfection, as we understand it, we still would not necessarily be the best looking, most athletic, or most artistic being in the universe. We will always be a unique mix of qualities and talents. Our task is to cherish what we are, and are becoming, rather than complain about what we are not.

Self-love and Self-esteem

In order to be mentally healthy, it is essential for us to cultivate positive feelings about ourselves. We all make mistakes and become disappointed in ourselves from time to time. For some it is difficult to forgive these errors and move on with life. The alternative, however, is self-loathing and fear, which can cripple our progression.

A talented college student sought help because of a self-image problem that had led to significant depression. Sue traced the origin of the problem back five years to a time when she thought a couple of young men from her high school had seen her through a window when she was undressed and admiring herself briefly in front of a mirror. Though she had no evidence that she was actually seen or that classmates had been told about it, she became extremely frightened about what people thought of her, and her self-image went into a tailspin. She imagined that people would think she was perverted, she said. Now, five years later, she was still avoiding contact with others. She looked away from people, afraid to see what might be in their eyes. She collected negative experiences as if they were stamps she could turn in for an important dividend and as proof that she was despicable to others.

Happily, a small part of Sue began to want to feel good again. She began of evaluate herself and discard some of her fears and self-loathing. She put her old negative experience behind her and started to live in the present. She practiced substituting positive thoughts about herself for ruminations about the past. To further strengthen her self-esteem, she began to treat herself as she might treat a good friend. I reminded her that the scriptural injunction "Love thy neighbour as thyself" (Matthew 19:19) presumes we have developed a good deal of self-love and self-esteem. She discovered that her capacity to care for others increased as she worked to improve her own self-image.

Sue learned an important principle. Loving ourselves is not selfish; rather, it is the only way to begin to really love others. I am astounded by the resistance I encounter about this concept. Loving oneself is mistakenly viewed as self-indulgent, childish, or conceited. While extreme self-love might lead to unhappy consequences, as extremes of any nature often do, it is unlikely that depressed people will go overboard in caring for themselves.

There is a dangerous, false belief about self-love which says that we must find someone to love *before* we can love ourselves or feel complete or satisfied. This idea only leads to dependency and unhappiness, however. Believing that we need someone else can spark a desperate search in which our standards are compromised because of an illusion. The truth is, no one else can really provide us with self-love, and potential worthy mates may sense our extreme neediness and self-doubt and avoid us. Further, we are likely to be overly sensitive of their shortcomings because of our insecurity and fear that if they are flawed, they cannot satisfy our many needs.

Self-love is an important prerequisite to a positive self-image. It develops over time, like any true and lasting love, through exercising kindness, forgiveness, and respect for ourselves.

Assertiveness and Self-esteem

A pattern of nonassertiveness that is found in many depressed individuals also contributes to low self-esteem. Imagine this scenario: While we are standing in a long line at a movie, someone cuts in front of us. Saying nothing can lead to self-doubt and negative thoughts, such as "It's okay for people to take advantage of me—I'm nobody important," or "I must look like a real chump if he dares push in front of me." Lack of assertiveness in such situations, where we do nothing to defend our position, can lead to our feeling put-down. When self-esteem is weakened, it becomes more difficult for us to be assertive next time, and a negative, self-perpetuating cycle is strengthened. Standing up for our rights in an appropriate manner, however, can promote an improvement in self-image. Saying, for example, "Excuse me, but the end of the line is forming back there," lets the intruder know we are unwilling to be used in this manner. Chances are other people in the line will show their approval too (especially those behind us), further bolstering our self-image.

Believing in oneself enough to stand up for legitimate rights is a cornerstone of self-esteem. The notion that we must defer to others in all situations is false and potentially harmful because it can signal that we are willing to be stepped on, like a door mat. Unfortunately, many people are willing to use door mats to cleanse their own soles.

Christ's admonition and example of service to others did not include being used by them against His will. For example, when Mary, His mother, apparently asked Him to provide wine for a wedding feast when hers ran out, He told her, "Mine hour is not yet come." He considered the needs of His ministry before responding to her request and performing His first recorded miracle. (See John 2:2-11.) And when a woman who had been suffering from a hemorrhage for twelve years reached for the hem of His garment to be healed, Jesus noticed strength passing from Him and inquired who had touched Him. His power might have healed many, destroyed the Roman legions, or changed the course of rivers, but it was kept for establishing His ministry, and He alone decided on its use. (Mark 5:25-34.) Jesus defended His personal rights and those of others as well.

Some individuals confuse assertiveness with aggressive, hostile, or demanding behavior. These are not models of healthy assertiveness. Assertiveness means asking for our fair share; it is an extension of the golden rule, asking to be treated by others with the respect we extend to them. It is essentially our way of saying, "I like me, and I deserve to be treated justly."

Working toward Self-esteem

Some people may think, "Well, that's fine for others, but I really haven't accomplished anything in my life to be proud of." (That in itself would make one someone special if it were true. I don't know of anyone who has done absolutely nothing.) When we are depressed, it is easier to focus on our shortcomings, but this cannot possibly build self-esteem.

How do we improve our self-image? Let's return to the four areas we discussed earlier: thoughts, environment, relationships, and physical needs.

1. *Thoughts:* Whose thoughts about us are the most important? If you think that I am a great roadshow director while I think I am a flop, which opinion carries the biggest punch? Remember, "As a man thinks, so is he."

Take out a piece of paper or an index card and

brainstorm with yourself for a minute (brainstorming means generating ideas without being critical). List your strengths, such as kindness, punctuality, courtesy, intelligence, creativity, dependability, physical stamina. Resist comparisons to other people; you don't have to be "the best" in order to take pride in your accomplishments. Many great athletes enter the Olympics, though only one gold medal is given in each event. If you are staring at a blank sheet after a few minutes, you are probably not being fair with yourself. Ask a friend to help you identify your strengths. Put this list in a prominent place where you will see it at least once a day. Memorize it and use it as a guide to reinforcing what's good in you. Rehearse these ideas when you are facing a challenge or feeling low. Perhaps you'll even feel good enough to add something once in a while. Add to the list as you feel better about yourself or receive positive strokes from others.

Learn to monitor your thoughts for distortions, such as labeling, overgeneralizations, *should* statements, and extreme thinking. Challenge these thoughts and replace them with more realistic ideas or with positive self-statements. Refuse to think negatively about yourself. Block out self-critical thoughts by saying no or "I don't want to think those kinds of thoughts anymore." You can also shake your head as if to say no. When you have practiced these techniques for a while, you can replace saying the words with thinking or imagining in your mind the word NO in big, bold letters.

Allow yourself to be imperfect, to be a "god in embryo." A popular poster shows a picture of a repentant-looking boy, with a caption that says, "Be patient, God isn't finished with me yet." Replace your self-criticism with positive thoughts such as this.

2. *Environment:* Look at how you spend your time, and every day plan at least two activities you can enjoy. Even if they seem minor, they will lift your spirits and help you feel good. Consider devoting some time each

day to something you do well, a task at work, a hobby or other pastime. If you're a good cook, create a favorite recipe and share it with someone who is appreciative. Accentuate your strengths and develop opportunities to excel. Everyone needs a chance to show off from time to time. Do nice things for yourself, such as taking a hot bath, listening to a favorite record, or changing the decor of your workspace. You deserve it, and your self-esteem will improve as you begin to treat yourself as somebody important. You have as much right to have fun as anybody else.

Another boost to self-esteem is to keep a prominent area in your home as a memento corner, where you display certificates, trophies, souvenirs, tickets, posters, and other reminders of positive experiences. Memory boxes can also be used for this purpose. Trophy cases at schools, churches, and clubs contain reminders of past glories to boost morale; this technique will work in your home, too. Create a trophy case or "hall of fame" with mementos from past accomplishments and positive experiences. Anything that makes you feel good can be included, from diplomas and ribbons to roadshow certificates (I've saved one the cast gave me for directing a roadshow almost ten years ago). Don't be shy about acknowledging what you have done, especially to yourself; it can promote self-confidence for future endeavors.

Read your patriarchal blessing frequently if you have received one. Realize that you are a child of God, and it is His desire to give you all that He has. Place evidences of your divine heritage and potential where you can see them; such as baptismal, marriage, and ordination certificates. These kinds of strategies are called "affirmations," for they remind or affirm for you in a positive way who you really are.

3. *Relationships:* Become involved with people who lift your spirits and have respect for you. Consider decreasing contact with friends who constantly point out our faults or try to keep you in a "one-down" position.

Nurturing and growthful relationships involve mutuality and sharing. Criticism, if given, should be provided in a positive way and followed by an increase of affection. (See D&C 121.) If you retain some friends only because you believe you couldn't live without them, you are wrong.

Practice assertiveness and don't be afraid to stand up for your fair share. Your self-respect will increase and so will the respect others show you, for mutual respect enhances self-esteem.

4. *Physical:* Take care of your body. Eat well, exercise, and get enough sleep. We are continually learning how important these three activities are to our well-being. Imbalances are not only symptoms of other difficulties, but often causes of distress and disease as well.

For better or worse, much of our self-esteem is focused on how we look, perhaps because our bodies are more observable than our thoughts, hopes, or dreams. Consider making efforts to improve your physical image. Don't be afraid to indulge yourself by losing weight, toning up, or getting a tan. Ask friends to tell you which of your outfits seem to be most flattering (and if you're daring, ask what is not flattering). Feeling confident about our appearance gives us an edge in many situations. I remember, for example, borrowing my brother's clothes for an important debate tournament because I respected his eye for fashion. Even though I was quivering and quaking on the inside, I projected a cool image on the outside.

Positive self-esteem does not mean we are totally pleased with every facet of our life. This would be impossible. A positive self-image is not a reward for perfection, but a powerful boost on the journey toward it.

Chapter 6

MOTIVATION
AND DEPRESSION

Sally was seriously depressed and unmotivated. She spent at least sixteen hours a day sleeping away her life. Therapy appointments were scheduled for nine o'clock to interrupt this pattern so that she would be up before noon at least one day a week. However, she left the therapist's office, returned home immediately, and went to bed. Sally was a champion at the game Eric Berne called "Why don't you . . . Yes, but . . ." in his book *Games People Play*. She would solicit suggestions or advice about her problems and then rattle off her prepared excuses: "Yes, but I'm too tired," or "Yes, but I'd be embarrassed," or "Yes, but I don't have the right clothes." This game destroyed her motivation and pushed away those whom she asked for help.

Sally played her game alone, without other people, as she languished in bed every day thinking of all the things she'd rather not do and all the excuses she needed for not doing them. One day, as she complained about the phone calls she had to make, how nervous she was about making them, and the disasters she anticipated if she did, the therapist had her go to his phone to make her calls. She was dumbfounded, but went to the phone, dialed the numbers, and handled herself well. In five minutes she transacted the important business she had been avoiding for weeks. She was surprised and pleased by the demonstration of what she could accomplish when pushed. After a few weeks of efforts like these, she began to do her own pushing, felt more motivated, and took control of her life, achieving the independence she had been denying herself.

Depressed individuals are not always seriously lacking in motivation as was Sally, nor is everyone who is short on motivation significantly depressed. Sally's story does, however, illustrate important principles about the interaction of motivation and depression. Sally was experiencing two of the most frequently reported symptoms of depression: *dysphoria,* which is a feeling of malaise or of things being not quite right, and *anhedonia,* a general lack of pleasure in any activity (literally, a lack of hedonism).

Because depression commonly lessens a person's ability to anticipate pleasure in advance, experience pleasure when it occurs, or relive it later, depressed individuals can feel devoid of any zest for life, even for activities that formerly brought them pleasure. The pattern of their thoughts and actions can actively maintain this state indefinitely. The primary motivation is mature, normal pleasure-seeking, and when this is stymied, depression results. No activity is fun, life has no point and no value, and consequently, depressed people feel like doing nothing.

A low level of motivation can initiate or accelerate a depressive, downward spiral. The resulting lack of energy leads the depressed individual to procrastinate even minor tasks (like making phone calls, for Sally), thus reinforcing negative thoughts and feelings of hopelessness. Things begin to pile up and feel overwhelming, the depression deepens, and the energy level spirals even further downward. This kind of cycle is self-perpetuating until one actively intervenes to counteract it.

The Effects of Procrastination

Procrastination is frequently one of the first signs that a person's motivation has begun to lag. Some tasks are inevitably more enjoyable than others, and most people can usually achieve a balance between "have-to's" and "want-to's," which helps them maintain motivation. Procrastination usually begins with "have-to's," and avoiding these mandatory tasks only increases the amount of negative energy we assign to them. It is as if we say, "Mowing the lawn must be a very terrible job, because I'll do anything to avoid it," and we thereby make it appear even more formidable. In this way, procrastination becomes a normal part of our day, even though it is an energy-sapping mind game that we play with ourselves.

To be successful, people have to be doers as well as thinkers. Procrastinators are often perpetual thinkers and worriers, unwilling to take action. In many ways, they are like the bride and her family in the children's story of "The Three Sillies." A young man went to meet the family of his bride-to-be and ask for permission to marry their daughter. As they all sat down to dinner, the young woman's mother noticed there was no jam for the rolls. She excused herself and went to the cellar to get some. When she did not return after several minutes had passed, the father left to see if he could help. Some time later, the young woman left the table to go find out what was keeping her father and mother so long.

The young man sat at the table alone for quite a while, waiting for them to return. Finally, he also went to the cellar. As he opened the cellar door, he heard wailing and moaning at the bottom of the stairs and rushed down to see what was the matter. There he found his bride-to-be and her parents crying hysterically, but he could see no injuries or threatening circumstances. The three all pointed to an ax lodged in the wood above the cellar door and the bride-to-be said, "What if we married, and had a son, and he grew up, and we were having dinner over here, and we sent him to the cellar for jam, and the ax fell on his head and killed him!" The young man, incredulous at their silly worries, reached up and took the ax down. He withdrew his promise of marriage and vowed he would return to her only if he met three people sillier than they were. Luckily for the young lady, he soon discovered several others with worries as ridiculous as hers, and he returned to her. Permitting thoughts and worries about the future to overwhelm us in this manner adds to our tendency to procrastinate, thus strengthening our depression.

Most people have had a few times in their lives when even though a situation seemed impossible, they were able to overcome challenges and have a successful experience. This could have been something as simple as getting the plaids to match while sewing a skirt with just barely enough fabric. Depression interferes with the ability to remember times when, under unfavorable circumstances, a positive outcome was reached. It therefore increases procrastination; it doesn't seem worthwhile to begin a task that may not be easily finished. Most people realize after completing a much delayed task that the worst part of it was over as soon as they began. We may also discover when the project is underway or completed that it was actually enjoyable. Procrastinators anticipate negative consequences and find it hard to focus on the possibility that the task may be less onerous than they have predicted.

Sooner or later procrastinators must face the consequences of inaction, and the experience is usually not positive. Being forced to do something at the last minute or by someone who uses coercion is unpleasant. The task then becomes the focus of negative thoughts and feelings, and resentment builds toward whatever compels us that may contribute to performing substandard work in a passive-aggressive manner.

Distortion and Motivation

Depressed individuals distort their thoughts about what is actually required of them. They exaggerate the complexity and riskiness of a task until it appears fearsome or insurmountable. For example, Sally feared calling her physician's receptionist for a referral to a specialist because she imagined that she would be insulted or made to feel stupid. She had no real basis for her fear, since no negative interactions had ever taken place. She had created imaginary obstacles to her progress and trapped herself within walls of hopelessness with her distortions (in this case, the distortion was her belief she could know the future and others' reactions to her). Real progress was achieved only when she acknowledged that the trap she had set was of her own creation and could be dismantled only by her.

Labeling is another thought distortion that contributes to low motivation, particularly the thought that we are a failure. Sam's story illustrates this problem. Sam had never learned much about baseball as a young boy; his father died when he was young and his brothers did not have much interest in teaching him about sports. He joined Little League because his friends did, but he had very little experience compared to the other boys. After two games he quit, discouraged, embarrassed, and dejected, a *failure*. He thought he was a physical reject and began to avoid any kind of athletics. Later in his life, he discovered by chance that he could enjoy and do well in another sport. Little by little, he tried other activities and developed a number of athletic interests. His motivation to participate in sports increased as he rejected the old label of failure.

Depressed people often expend a great deal of mental energy (which they are usually lacking to begin with), in avoiding a task or obligation. They generate explanations and excuses; they spend valuable time worrying about the consequences of their inaction, and, of course, they frequently bear a burden of guilt. More energy is spent thinking in this manner than the project itself would have required.

Memory for negative events is sharper during periods of depression, and any negative occurrences, whether real or imagined, are distorted and magnified. Preoccupation with how others act, conjecture about what they might be thinking, and our own aches and pains accentuate the possible distress or discomfort of any action. Sally demonstrated this by playing "Why don't you . . . Yes, but . . . " with people who were trying to help her. She focused on the liabilities rather than the possibilities of action, and instead of being a trouble-shooter, she became a trouble-finder.

Another factor that leads to decreased motivation is that one's ability to cope with frustration decreases with depression. Things that are normally accomplished with ease may become difficult because concentration and motor skills are impaired to some degree. Anger and frustration are turned inward because of these changes. Thoughts like "I'll never try that again" or "I can forget calligraphy—I've just lost my touch," intensify depressed feelings and decrease motivation.

Depression works in all these ways to block motivation, and that, of course, keeps us depressed. The ability to anticipate or experience pleasure decreases, as does frustration tolerance. Worry, guilt, self-criticism, and recall of negative consequences increase. Who wouldn't feel like giving up under these circumstances? Fortunately, by changing thoughts and actions we can increase feelings of motivation. Sometimes people roll their eyes in disbelief when someone starts to talk about "the power of positive thinking." The principle is a correct one, however, validated by both experience and research. It is particularly important to try to focus one's thoughts and actions in a positive manner when trying to increase motivation.

Effort and Patience

There is a natural ebb and flow of energy in everyone's life. Some days you feel strong enough to clean your whole house or finish the quarterly report; some days even minimal tasks leave you feeling drained. We can learn to take advantage of these normal changes by creative scheduling and flexibility in activity patterns. Depression, however, often changes this rhythm. The tides of motivation seem to be constantly low, and at times life cannot be put on hold until we feel like being active again.

Motivation is paradoxical: it is increased by *initiating* positive activity. Simply waiting to feel motivated is often fruitless and frustrating. Alma, in the Book of Mormon, offered a prescription for increasing faith that is also applicable to motivation. He challenged his readers to exercise even a particle of faith, to nurture it, and to enjoy the feelings that it would create. (See Alma 32:27-33.) Beginning small, positive activities will increase motivation in the same way as exercising a bit of faith enlarges it. The catches for many people are (1) the effort required to begin, and (2) exercising patience as their efforts start to "take root."

Today's world promotes the notion of instant, no-effort remedies such as diet pills, fabulous physiques in less than three days, and get-rich-quick schemes. Many people would rather try to find an easy way out than exercise self-discipline. In spite of the claims of our "instant society," however, natural laws are still operating. One of those laws of physics states that the greatest effort is expended in initially moving a stationary object; after it is rolling, less energy is required to keep it going. The initial efforts to increase our own activity are usually the hardest; it is a struggle to get going. Perhaps President

Spencer W. Kimball provided the most simple and sound advice on increasing motivation by making the phrase "Do it" popular.

Another principle that is common knowledge to farmers and gardeners, but resisted by the general population, is sowing and reaping. Food and flowers do not spring up from the ground without cultivation and patience—at least they have not done so since Eden. There must first be an investment of seed, effort, and time for things to grow. A further example of this concept is priming a pump to create a flow from a well. Some well pumps require that water first be poured down them to create the pressure gradients necessary to draw more water from the underground store. Using water serves to create more water, just as planting seeds will lead to a crop with a greater abundance of seeds in the fruit of flowers. Sometimes we have to *do* in order to feel more like *doing*.

It is not the complexity of the activity that is most important. Practically any activity is better than doing nothing. Even doing a load of wash chases the blues away for some people by giving them a sense of accomplishment. Develop a list of little things that bring you pleasure, and keep it handy for times you feel unmotivated. Then, if you're down, get up, get dressed, and try something for a few minutes. Use the list or think of a few other minor projects (ten minutes or less) and complete them. This will give you a boost and a sense of mastery and is an important precursor to feelings of greater motivation.

Successfully completing a few things increases energy, enthusiasm, and the probability we will take on a little more. Professionals who design tests understand this principle. Tests begin with questions that are easy and then increase in difficulty as the test continues because research has established that test takers score higher if they can easily complete the first answers. We can organize our time like this too. Some people do well by attacking the most difficult thing first, but the majority do better by warming up. Like athletes, we're less likely to "pull a muscle" and drop out of competition if we're warmed up.

Impatience can also drain off energy and decrease motivation. Some tasks cannot be completed at once but require a sustained effort over a long period of time. Life consists of a myriad of activities, from baking cookies to finishing postgraduate work. Each day there are a variety of things to do, some of which can be finished today, some of which will take years to complete, and many others in between. Patience contributes to motivation by decreasing the pressures we sometimes unrealistically impose on ourselves and others.

Break It Down

An old riddle provides some insight on how to increase motivation, particularly for the big jobs: "How do you eat an elephant?" "One bite at a time!"

When energy and enthusiasm are depleted by depression, even a small task can seem as overwhelming as eating an elephant. Break it down into parts that you *can* achieve in a relatively short period of time, and then work on it. This is a principle of eternal progression, and it applies to everything we do, large or small. We learn "line upon line, precept upon precept." Journeys begin with steps, towers are made of individual bricks, and our accomplishments are a series of smaller efforts. This book was written over a period of months—some days ten pages, some days ten words.

It is easy to to become overwhelmed by our thoughts. Try this experiment: Imagine a large table. Now place on this table the food you ate today, add yesterday's, then the food you ate the day before, and so on. It doesn't take long to feel full or become nauseated from these thoughts. This kind of mind game occurs when we try to do everything at once or expend energy worrying about the next step while we are doing the current one.

Focusing only on large projects is overwhelming. Soon, even the small tasks seem like incredible chores, and getting out of bed to face the world becomes burdensome. With our thoughts and inaction, we have created negative feelings and become more depressed. This is a good time to remember the elephant. A large project has many facets, and energy can be conserved by shuttling between tasks that contribute to its completion. Think about what you could do in the next five minutes to move toward the goal. Take a small bite and enjoy.

Tasks can be made to appear less overwhelming by limiting the time spent working on them each day. This is a particularly helpful technique if you procrastinate getting started on something until you have the time to complete it. Make realistic goals; try telling yourself, "I'll shovel snow for one-half hour" or "If I clean until four o'clock, I'll quit for the day." It's better for your morale to be realistic and achieve the mark than to be idealistic and fall short, especially since depression increases sensitivity to defeat. Do something rewarding after completing the onerous activity. Call a friend, read some poetry, or take a walk and enjoy the scenery to strengthen your sense of well-being and reinforce your accomplishment.

"Have To's"

The job or task itself can seem unmotivating, particularly if it feels like a "have-to." For instance, it's easy to think we're *only* a Primary teacher, ward librarian, or activity coordinator, a position that anybody could fill. Why invest a lot in it? These thoughts are certainly demoralizing and can be destructive to our self-esteem. Think back on your life. Who has most influenced you outside your family? Chances are it was a teacher, not the President of the United States, or your bishop, or a General Authority, or someone in a high status position. Yet our typical thoughts about teaching assignments and other low-profile tasks are negative. Such assignments are passed off as dull and insignificant.

The bishop asked Ruth to teach the Guide Patrol, a group of boys who took pride in how quickly they could wear teachers out (and they were going for a new record). It would have been easier for Ruth to be a baby sitter, not try to teach anything, and get through the forty-five minutes until the little gremlins went home. She had higher hopes, though. She wasn't "just another teacher." She became *their* teacher, not the first week, probably not the first month, but through a series of efforts both large and small. As the boys grew up and had the chance to address the ward before leaving for missions, marriage, or school, several of them remembered Ruth for her courage and love. Now each time I accept a teaching assignment, I try to remember her example to bolster my own motivation. A whimsical thought about attitude in situations like these is "There are no small parts, only small actors."

Everything we do fills some role or purpose, whether it is cleaning house, herding sheep, teaching college, or digging ditches. Our own opinion of its value will make the most difference in how motivated we feel about pursuing it. Believing that a task or assignment is meaningless is self-defeating and demoralizing. Perhaps it is better to be honest and decline rather than become caught in this type of depressive cycle.

Criticism and Motivation

Criticism—whether of self or of others—seldom contributes to increasing motivation. It does, however, feed depression. Let's eavesdrop on an inner dialogue: "Get to work on that report. You always put things off until the last minute. You're a failure. You'll never get it done." Did you feel more or less motivated as you read this? Most of us feel more anxious and would be less likely to take on the task. The truth is, criticism of ourselves, family, friends, or associates can often be the *least* helpful and productive way to get something done. There are examples of the "drill sergeant" style being used successfully by a parent, an athletic coach, a debate teacher, or others, but unless you are absolutely certain that you respond well to criticism, it is better to use another way to get yourself going.

Resist the temptation to constantly evaluate what you do by comparing yourself with others or even what you may have done a few days ago. Today you are different. Give yourself credit for whatever you do, because your effort counts. You will not always succeed, but you will learn if you try. If basketball teams just quit playing when they lost a game, it would be a short season. Sometimes the league leaders lose to the last-place team. Perhaps the losing team has an off-night, players are out with injuries, or the other team is just hot. The fact is that this year's second-rate players may be the national champions next year if they just keep trying to improve and don't walk off the floor.

At times, all of us commit to doing more than we can do. Feeling overwhelmed can precede depression and the loss of energy. It can be exciting to accept a challenge to do more than usual from time to time, but we do have limits. Develop the skill of anticipating how much you will be able to accomplish. Your primary stewardship is to take care of yourself, and this may mean saying no to someone. Bosses, friends, Church leaders, and families all have requests for us, and ideally their wishes would balance with those of others and the natural rhythms of our own life, but since they are not privy to all of the other demands on us, they may ask too much. It is up to us to set limits and keep our balance. If you consistently wake up in the morning feeling dreadful about the day's activities, it's time to review your priorities and commitments before you engage in destructive self-criticism that will sap any energy you may have left.

Techniques for Increasing Motivation

Some people have used the following techniques successfully in increasing their motivation:

1. *Test out the assumption that you can't do something.* Break it into small parts and try a piece of it. Self-efficacy, the belief that you can have impact on or change your world, leads to greater accomplishment than a negative "can't" attitude, which stops you before you have begun. Many "can'ts" are actually "won't try's."

2. *Focus on what can be gained from effort rather than on total victory.* Not everyone succeeds one hundred percent of the time, and valuable lessons can be learned even if the objective is not totally achieved. Human nature seems to dictate that as a project's chances for success appear to decrease, effort also decreases. Often this decision is based on extreme thinking: if you are not going to be totally successful, why try? Looking at the world as all black or all white, as a success or as a failure, will prevent a lot of positive growth by promoting fear of failure and restricting those activities you will be willing to engage in. History is replete with famous "failures." Columbus failed to discover a new route to India; Edison failed hundreds of times before creating a filament for the light bulb. It is almost impossible to think of anyone who has succeeded quickly or totally at what they set out to do. Life is not a winner-take-all contest. Motivation can be increased by focusing on growth and effort instead of winners and losers.

3. *Shorten feedback loops.* When you feel unmotivated, tackle a few projects that can bring pleasure and satisfaction quickly, such as writing a letter, fixing a door, exercising, or helping someone else with a small project. This establishes a connection between action and positive results, thereby increasing motivation.

4. *Remember that variety is the spice of life and a boon to motivation.* Sometimes shuttling between projects that require different skills provides a needed break. For example, employees whose jobs allow greater diversity report

higher job satisfaction and are more productive than are workers whose jobs are more monotonous. Organize your time to provide diversity when possible.

5. *Keep a "have done" list.* It is common to hear a depressed individual say, "I haven't done anything all day." This type of extreme thinking can be corrected by making a brief list of things to do and using it to organize time and reinforce what is accomplished. At the end of the day it becomes a "have done" list and helps provide solid, positive feedback. Collecting this evidence over a period of a week is even more convincing. If you tend to get carried away with lists, start with only five things to do and don't add anything else until you have finished one of them. The number of items remains constant at five, thus offering variety and a chance for you to set priorities without becoming overwhelmed.

6. *Keep track of motivation in your journal.* A journal can provide self-reinforcing evidences of what you accomplish. Looking back over the entries can give you insight into the natural ebbs and flows of your energy and help you identify ways to organize your time and maximize your efficiency. It can also remind you of times you overcame difficult circumstances to achieve your goals. You can compare comments about the anticipated difficulty of a project and the pleasure you expect to derive from it with your reactions after it is completed, and thus discover how realistic your thoughts have been. Individuals who lack motivation and use this technique often find that they overestimate the difficulty of projects and underestimate the pleasure they feel when they are completed. Their energy increases as they view life more realistically.

7. *Avoid the workaholic syndrome.* Some people who worry about flagging motivation are actually workaholics. Sooner or later, their bodies cry out for a rest, and pushing even harder only makes matters worse. All of us need vacations from working from time to time. The workaholic is annoyed by these interruptions or becomes

anxious that he will never have the energy to return to the work. What could be a re-creational respite turns into a downward spiral of negative and self-condemning thoughts. Try taking a few days out for a *real* rest. Resolve to use one hundred percent of the time enjoying the feelings of relaxation. Like a good night's rest, a vacation can restore your ability to concentrate and increase your energy.

8. *Avoid the college-student syndrome.* Students often study ferociously several days before an exam and then slack off until just before the next test. Not only is this a poor way to study (usually retention of material learned in this way is impaired), but their lives can begin to feel like a roller coaster. Because they work so hard for a few days, the rest seems to be deserved. Unfortunately, however, total rest continues until there is another crisis, and the cycle becomes self-perpetuating. Try to remember Aesop's fable of the tortoise and the hare. Slow and steady not only can win many races, but it can also keep you from collapsing from exhaustion. Schedule a fair balance of work and play.

9. *Use positive mental imagery to increase motivation.* This is done by creating a mental picture of what you would feel like if you accomplished your goal. The power of imagery seems to increase as the mental image is elaborated upon and anticipated. For instance, if the house needed painting, I might conjure up an image of the completed project, enjoying the feelings of pride in my work, anticipating others admiring it or even the relief of having it done. Maxwell Maltz, in his classic book *Psychocybernetics*, demonstrates the effectiveness of this technique in many situations.

10. *Make a balance sheet for the task you're procrastinating.* Listing the advantages and disadvantages of inaction can help clarify the reasons you may be avoiding something and offer a more positive perspective. Putting the ideas on paper often makes it more feasible to contend with them rationally, too.

Chapter 7

PERFECTION: A PROCESS

Perhaps no teaching about the nature of God has been as revolutionary as the Latter-day Saint doctrine of man's divine potential. Simply stated, it is, "As man is, God once was; as God is, man may become." Perfection, becoming like the gods, is our ultimate goal, and this earth life was provided to prepare us to become heirs to our Father's kingdom. Many people, however, seem to misunderstand this principle and how it applies to this life.

Some Latter-day Saints feel like failures because they believe they must meet or exceed during their earthly mortality the level of perfection attained by the Savior. Others cite scriptural evidence to support this lofty, though unrealistic, goal. A pattern of self-condemnation because of faults and imperfections seldom provides motivation or inspiration to strive for excellence, however. It is more likely to be demoralizing and to invite depression. A review of some key scriptures and the life of Jesus places the journey toward perfection in its true perspective.

One of the most frequently quoted scriptures on perfection is part of Christ's Sermon on the Mount: "Be ye therefore perfect, even as your Father which is in heaven

is perfect." (Matthew 5:48.) Christ repeated this commandment on the American continent following His resurrec-
tion when He said, "Therefore I would that ye should be
perfect even as I, or as your Father who is in heaven is
perfect." (3 Nephi 12:48.) On both occasions Jesus had
been teaching many important gospel principles to the
people, and the pursuit of perfection and godliness was
central to His message. His ultimate goal for us is perfection. The misunderstanding arises as to what we are actually expected to achieve during mortality.

A closer look at each of these scriptures clarifies the
nature of the "perfection" that we are commanded to
seek in this life. The King James Version of the Bible
published by the Church in 1979 includes the words
"complete, finished, fully developed" as alternative
translations from Greek texts of the word *perfect* in
Matthew 5:48. Substituting those words in the context of
the scripture, it appears that Christ was exhorting the
people to live the commandments until they achieved
godhood.

Christ's message to those on the American continent
was strikingly similar to His teachings from the Sermon
on the Mount. His statement about perfection on that
occasion, "Therefore I would that ye should be perfect,"
also appears to be His wish for us to obtain perfection
and share in the glory of God. Perfection, to be like God,
is the goal toward which we travel in mortality.

It is useful to examine the way in which the Savior obtained perfection and godhood in order to gain an understanding of the nature of the process and our own
struggles in this life.

Elder James E. Talmage discussed the way that
Christ attained earthly perfection in his book *Jesus the
Christ.* In describing the early life of Christ, Elder Talmage wrote: "In such simplicity is the normal, natural
development of the Boy Jesus made clear. He came
among men to experience all the natural conditions of
mortality; He was born as truly a dependent, helpless

babe as is any other child; His infancy was in all common features as the infancy of others; His boyhood was actual boyhood, His development was as necessary and as real as that of all children. Over His mind had fallen the veil of forgetfulness common to all who are born to earth, by which the remembrance of primeval existence is shut off. The Child grew, and with growth there came to Him expansion of mind, development of faculties, and progression in power and understanding. His advancement was from one grace to another, not from gracelessness to grace; from good to greater good, not from evil to good; from favor with God to greater favor, not from estrangement because of sin to reconciliation through repentance and propitiation." (Deseret Book Company, 1982 ed., pp. 105-6; 1971 ed., pp. 111-12.)

The Savior grew in the same way that each of us in mortality must grow, line upon line and precept upon precept. The apostle John recorded this pattern of growth: "I, John, saw that he received not of the fulness at the first, but received . . . grace for grace until he received a fulness; and thus he was called the Son of God, because he received not of the fulness at the first." (Doctrine and Covenants 93:12-14.) Jesus became the Savior because He grew in the direction of His Father and earned perfection and godhood in this manner.

Jesus was, of course, also the literal son of God, and He therefore received a tremendous genetic and biological endowment to begin His earthly journey. For thirty years He was taught by Joseph and Mary, the two best mortals available to teach Him about humanity and His unique spiritual heritage. Even with a heritage greater than that of any mortal, He still required thirty years of learning and growth before He began to perform His sacred ministry.

Who would criticize the Savior for taking so long to perfect Himself? Yet, when we are in a down mood, we feel no qualms about cursing and nagging ourselves for not completing our growth on the same schedule He did, by age thirty—or even earlier. Though the process of perfection is similar for everyone, it is important to keep a proper perspective by remembering that Christ possessed qualities beyond a mortal man's from birth. Is it fair to compare ourselves with Him when we do not have the divine lineage He had nor direct access to heavenly tutors as He did?

Comparing ourselves to Christ's perfection is like a couple who have been married only two years comparing their marital happiness and success with that of President Kimball and his wife, who were successfully married for over fifty years. It is not only unrealistic; it also leads to frustration, impatience, and dissatisfaction between the couple. They lose the proper perspective on their relationship and the progress of their marriage. Camilla Kimball, speaking candidly about the early years of her marriage, stated, "He wasn't the prophet when I married him." Choosing impossible standards with which to compare ourselves invites depression. It is much more helpful and realistic to use the Lord or the Prophet as *examples* of the goal toward which we are traveling rather than using them as *standards* against which we compare ourselves or our progress.

Eternal Progression

The system of achieving godhood that was presented in the great councils in heaven during premortality was not designed to be finished here in mortality; therefore, few, if any, will experience total perfection in this mortal phase of life. The Prophet Joseph Smith taught that the greater part of the work on our exaltation and perfection would be done in the spirit, not in mortality. "It is not all to be comprehended in this world; it will be a great work to learn our salvation and exaltation even beyond the grave." (*Teachings of the Prophet Joseph Smith*, p. 348.) There will be work to do in the spirit after death, in the millennial world, in the "little season" that precedes final judgment, and perhaps even beyond that.

Here, in this life, we start the journey toward godhood and set our feet upon the path that will eventually lead us to perfection. We cannot expect to build the perfection we are seeking in this imperfect world, which is so full of turmoil and commotion that the world cannot accommodate perfection. Enoch and the citizens of his city, for instance, were taken from the earth when they reached a certain level of righteousness. Actually, the earth itself will need to be perfected prior to its becoming the home for perfected celestial beings. (See Doctrine and Covenants 130:9.) If you are not perfect, realize that you are not really expected to be perfect in all things yet. It is very important to learn how to be happy enough with ourselves to sustain the motivation necessary to continue on the path to perfection during this life.

Perfection: A Mirage

Mirages occur when our senses are tricked into seeing something that really does not exist. Thirsty desert travelers have experienced seeing water in the sand ahead, only to find more sand when they reached the spot where the water appeared to be. Perfection in this world is also a mirage. From a distance we imagine that something or someone is perfect, but on closer inspection, the cracks, blotches, and glitches become clear. Perfection, like beauty, can only be in the eyes of the beholder and is frequently a matter of personal opinion and preference. What is a perfect day? a perfect vacation? a perfect dinner? Each person's answers would be different, and they would each be right, at least for the person himself. Perhaps we misuse an eternal principle by trying to apply it to things in this world.

The reality is that perfection in this world does not exist. A declaration that something perfect has been discovered only means that current thinking or technology is not powerful enough to detect the variation or imperfection that actually exists. For example, scientists are preparing to build a new telescope so powerful, it is said, that they will be able to observe from earth the light of a candle on the moon. Because of their unique design, the telescope's mirrors will have to be aligned one hundred times a second by as little as one one-thousandth the width of a human hair through the use of a computer. Though the telescope will be fifty to one hundred times stronger than any existing instrument, however, it will not be perfect.

Because man is constantly expanding his abilities, knowledge, and technology, his concept of perfection also changes. As we grow in the gospel, our capacity to approximate the perfection of the gods expands in a similar manner. Perfection in this mortal world, however, is impossible.

A dangerous, emotional pit develops when people make constant, unrealistic demands for immediate perfection on themselves and have inaccurate expectations about the rewards of righteous living. When trapped in these thoughts, they begin to believe that mortality is a series of inescapable frustrations and disappointments. They feel doomed because of their imperfections and angry because life does not necessarily become easier when they try harder to keep the commandments. Such thoughts also create depression, which further paralyzes progression and breeds rebellion and more anger, thus taking them even farther away from the path leading toward perfection and exaltation.

Kent became trapped in this pit of perfectionism because of his inaccurate expectations about the relationship between perfecting oneself and earthly rewards for righteous living. He had tried to do everything he believed he was supposed to do; as a young man he had been active in his priesthood quorums, a seminary officer, a diligent missionary, and a conscientious member of his student ward. He had dated the "right" girls, maintained his morality while dating, married in the temple, and started his family. His wife, however, began to lose interest in religion and refused to attend church with him. At first, he hoped her feelings would change if he were patient and kindly; but as the months went on, the distance between them increased. David sought counsel from a church leader, who naively pointed to several minor flaws in his adherence to orthodoxy and suggested that these problems might be contributing to his troubles at home. Following their interview, David resolved to try harder. Several months later, however, though he had followed his leader's advice and resolved his own minor problems, his wife asked for a divorce. David became desperately depressed because he had hoped that by being faithful and keeping the commandments, he could hold his young family together. He lashed out in anger because of disappointment and pain and ultimately left the Church.

David's faithfulness and obedience were commendable, but his attitude and expectations were unrealistic. His expectation that if he further perfected himself all else would automatically fall into place was false. He had, for example, failed to consider his wife's free agency, which allowed her to choose not to follow gospel principles. He had forgotten that though he could travel the road to perfection himself, he could not control the path that those around him chose to take. This realization is often very painful. As the prophet Lehi learned in his dream, families and friends do not always travel in the same directions.

The Millstone of Criticism

Criticism is often a harbinger of depression and despair. It does not offer much assistance in our struggle for perfection, since it only tells us what not to do and provides little positive direction or incentive. Since it is considered impolite to unkindly criticize others, can it be any better to unkindly criticize ourselves? The choice of chronic criticism as a tool to modify and improve ourselves has predictable, negative consequences.

Observing the consequences of criticism illustrates

how unproductive it really is. For example, observe an interaction between a parent and her son on report card day:

"This is the worst report card I have ever seen."

"But Mom!"

"Don't you 'But' me, young man. You are grounded until you can improve your grades, and that's final."

This dialogue is vintage criticism of the most destructive kind. Let's analyze it carefully to understand its impact.

In the first line, the report card, and by simple implication the child, is negatively labeled. He is the "worst." The child may be trying to provide an explanation in his response, but his mother's next sentence tells him she wants no further information from him because the whole thing is completely clear to her. Her concluding comment tells him that she doesn't care how long it takes him to shape up but it will happen, and he will do it or suffer until it occurs.

All of the statements made by the parent in this example are critical and negative evaluations. The boy hears that he is terrible, not that his grades are terrible. These labels do not motivate him to change, but are more likely to generate frustration, rebellion, and anger. The mother has not bothered to try to discover what his problem is or to problem-solve with him about how to correct it. She has responded as if the grades themselves were the problem, which is usually not the case.

Each day hundreds of destructive exchanges like this one also take place *within* us. They are often based on real situations from our past when we have been criticized. All of these old experiences and messages become condensed into patterns of thought that have been labeled the "critical parent" by transactional analysts in books such as *I'm OK, You're OK* and *Games People Play*. These negative messages and labels, derived from an actual critical parental or authority figure, are usually carried inside us into adulthood without revision or update and become the source of our inner criticism. The result is a kind of war within ourselves because these messages often contain unrealistic or outdated ideas that can conflict with our progression as an adult. The only way to deal with this inner critical dialogue is to question the messages of the "critical parent," which are usually a tangle of conflicting rules by which we are trying to live.

For an entire day really listen to your inner dialogue and see how many times you hear someone else's values and beliefs in sentences that begin, "I should . . . ," "I ought to . . . ," or "I must" do this or that. This exercise, and listening for other forms of self-criticism, will place in perspective the impact of the "critical parent" on your moods and thinking. Remember, it is not you who are speaking when the thought is introduced by "should," "ought," or "must." If the idea or value is a part of you, it will be expressed as "I want to . . ." or "I will . . ."

Though no one seems to remember having benefited from nagging lectures when they were given by our parents, many people naively employ self-nagging as a technique for self-improvement. Being critical or hard on ourselves does not speed the journey toward perfection. Though it is healthy and mature to recognize our mistakes, it is destructive to continue to punish ourselves for them.

A new style of thinking can be fostered in order to quit nagging and hassling ourselves in ways that feed and maintain depression. It is possible to be honest and tactful with ourselves in the same way we might be with a good friend, and, in that way, we protect our self-esteem. Engaging in honest self-evaluation is completely different from self-criticism. Thinking and planning in an uncritical fashion provides information and direction. Unlike criticism, this process does not undermine the motivation we need to accomplish our goals. The object of self-evaluation is improvement and growth through self-awareness and self-acceptance.

We are much more likely to shape our behavior in

positive ways through a supportive inner dialogue than by engaging in self-criticism. Find out how well you accomplish this by monitoring your thoughts and noticing how many positive affirmations—pats, strokes, or compliments—you give yourself or allow others to give you. Unfortunately there is a large gap here for many of us. Other people will provide more than enough criticism to keep us humble, but who builds us up and cheers us on in our quest for perfection? Each individual serves as his most important cheerleader in the game of life and improves his chances of winning by the kindness and enthusiasm he invests in himself. His attitude and actions also set a pattern for others who interact with him to follow.

In many restaurants where live music is part of the dinner, the musicians place a large container for tips within easy reach of the restaurant patrons. The experienced performer does not let the container start out empty. He places a few dollar bills in it to signal to the listener what he is worth. He knows that people are more likely to place bills in a container that already has paper money in it than one with quarters, dimes, or nickels. When the musician sets the tone for how others will treat him by salting the container with greenbacks, he is, in a very direct manner, engaging in self-affirmation.

Every day each of us, without thinking about it, sets the trend by which others will treat us and by the way in which we are either kind or cruel to ourselves. When people respond poorly to you, it may be because they, mistakenly but sincerely, believe you really do like the dried-out, burnt end of the roast because they never see you eating anything else at family dinners.

Growing Toward Perfection

Discipline comes from the word *disciple,* which means a follower of someone or some principle. This concept is commonly thought to be synonymous with punishment and is resisted as one might resist a spanking. Discipline, however, has to do with who we are following or modeling our lives after, rather than with punishment. Members of the Church, of course, try to follow our Eternal Father and His Son as well as the examples of the prophets and other great individuals. We are literally following the pathway God himself trod. God has experienced the struggle toward perfection; He understands the magnitude of the task and also the time it takes to achieve it. The prophets of today are struggling along with us to endure to the end, and they are busy working out their own salvation. We do not travel alone.

A few years ago the book *Jonathan Livingston Seagull,* by Richard Bach, became a very popular bestseller, read and discussed by millions. The story, a simple one with almost universal appeal, deals with the process of perfecting oneself.

The story tells of a seagull, Jonathan, who tires of following the fishing fleet and eating the garbage left behind as the men clean their catch. Against the advice of his peers, he leaves the daily routines of the flock and seeks his own self-development and enrichment. Jonathan was, perhaps, a pioneer in the "do your own thing" movement. His "thing" was learning to fly higher and faster than anyone else had ever gone before or even believed possible. The story chronicles his experiences of learning. He continues to grow and achieve despite his errors and failures because he tries to learn as much as possible from them. He recovers from his crashes and close calls and tries again. After much effort, Jonathan eventually masters the art of feathered flight and becomes perfect, as far as those principles are concerned. He is able to fly or travel from place to place in an instant, just by thinking about it.

Two important insights into the process of perfection can be gained from Jonathan's story. First, success and failure go hand in hand. One cannot be had without the other. In making attempts to grow, a person inevitably crashes; and only when he picks himself up and persists can he progress. Second, in the story of Jonathan Livingston Seagull, perfection does not have an end point. There is no place where heavenly gates part, trumpets sound, and a powerful voice announces that Jonathan has made it. Joseph Smith also taught the concept of "eternal progression," explaining that even the gods continue to grow in glory through their creations. Perfection is a continual process, not a finish line on a race course. Our concern in this life is with being on the right course and moving with reasonable speed toward the goal, not with who is in front of us or behind us. Our journey toward perfection and glory will continue into the eternities.

Faith is required to commit ourselves to embark on the journey toward godhood. Uncertainty about the existence of God and His plan for us keeps some from making a commitment. Others, who have faith in God, hesitate because they have doubts about their ability to finish the journey, or what really awaits them after they have completed this life. These questions must be answered by each of us as individuals. It is very difficult to continue through our journey in life on the testimony of others. Resolving these issues is critical to the ability to enjoy our progress through life.

We can also become overwhelmed by the multitude of commandments and suggestions that have been given about how to live life. Some commandments, such as payment of tithing or observing the Word of Wisdom, are relatively clear and we can gauge our level of compliance. With other commandments, such as "love your enemies," it is harder to measure our progress. Some members of the Church become overwhelmed and depressed by the complexity and demands of totally living their religion.

Motivation for living the gospel can be increased by breaking down into small steps the enormous, life-long journey toward perfection. For instance, it is impossible to perfectly love our enemies tomorrow, but we can speak kindly to the neighbor we have been refusing to speak to during our feud about the cherry tree. Like

Jonathan, we will become perfect by taking small steps and moving forward.

As We Think, So We Become

An individual's thoughts determine what he is and what he will become. People can think their way into and out of disastrous depressions, fits of anxiety, episodes of love and hate, and even the kingdom of God. Because thinking appears to be an effortless and natural process, it is easy to become lazy and complacent with our thoughts and thus become easy prey to the negativism so prevalent in the world around us. It is a mistake to think that the only reality is the sort of thing that makes headlines or the evening news.

Some people seem to fear that they will create a fantasy kingdom out of the fluff and clouds of beautiful thoughts if they do not attend to the pain, inhumanity, and unrighteousness of the world. Unfortunately, they often lose their perspective and develop eyes that see only the rocks and ruts of the path to perfection. They also lose the ability to lift their eyes to enjoy any of the beauty along the road or see the goal in the distance.

A priesthood quorum lesson about fellowshipping those around us led to a discussion of how Latter-day Saints are viewed by those with whom they associate. Each quorum member experienced being thought of as pure and saintly by his nonmember peers, sometimes in reverence, sometimes as a subject of ridicule. In comparison to his fellow quorum members, however, each man felt he was lacking greatly in the attributes of godliness. Of course, neither of these situations presented a balanced picture of their degree of perfection. Comparisons with others almost always distort the picture. A true perspective of the journey toward perfection must take into account our own individual struggles and strengths.

A short prayer has been written that places the struggle for perfection in its proper perspective: "Heavenly Father, I am not as good as I could be, I am not as good as I should be, but I am better than I was. Amen." It is important to recognize the progress that we do make on the road to perfection. If the rewards are to be enjoyed only when the job is completely done, then Latter-day Saints are no better off than members of other religious groups who believe they must wait to experience joy in the hereafter. God made his plan for us clear when he said, "Men are, that they might have joy." (2 Nephi 2:25.) Recognizing our accomplishments provides needed boosts as we journey through life.

Doing Our Best

For more than seventy-five years, millions of Boy Scouts have recited their oath, which begins, "On my honor I will do my best . . ." Leaders of the Church were so impressed by the scouting program and its philosophy that they adopted it to supplement the Aaronic Priesthood program just three years after the movement came to the United States from its birthplace in England. The Scout Oath does not promise perfection, but a genuine effort to do one's best. Those who work with young men in scouting or priesthood can attest to the tremendous growth that occurs while pursuing this commitment.

Doing our best is an attainable goal, and letting go of the wish and fantasy of immediate perfection allows us to experience greater freedom and joy. Most people can identify times when they have put forth their best efforts, and they know that they can enjoy feelings of satisfaction even when they fall short of their ultimate goals. Striving for excellence instead of perfection allows us to have daily victories as we do our best, instead of waiting through the eternities for elusive perfection. Resolving to do our best also anchors any comparisons we make to the person we are really trying to better, *ourself*. Our best will grow each time we outdo ourselves and move us closer to our eternal goals. In this sense we can all become winners as we experience joy and fulfillment from doing our personal best.

David O. McKay often recalled these words carved in a stone that was part of a building he saw while a missionary in Scotland: "What e'er thou art, act well thy part." He challenged members of the Church to live by this creed and perform their tasks in life as well as they could. A few years ago an alert missionary who had heard this message from President McKay noticed that the building was about to be torn down, and he took steps to obtain the stone for the Church so that its message could continue to inspire those who passed by it to do their best.

At a stake conference some years ago, Jessie Evans Smith, the wife of President Joseph Fielding Smith, told a congregation she had persuaded her husband, who was to speak next, to tell them when the world would end. Standing at the pulpit and looking solemnly out into the faces in the congregation, President Smith said, "The world will end tomorrow." Following a tremendous, audible gasp and what seemed like an eternity to the audience, he explained that for any of us, this life could end tomorrow through illness or accident. Our task was to live life in the present and do our best today in order to be prepared for tomorrow.

Those who are willing to commit their lives to the Lord, and to struggle consistently to keep the commandments and the covenants they make while in this life, will over the next thousand years or so become prepared for perfection and godhood. This is God's ultimate goal for His children, and it will be obtained in a gradual process of which this earth life is only a portion.

Those who spend their time stewing, fretting, and suffering self-criticism and doubt will be prepared only for an eternal world of worry and hassle, for that is the heaven for which they have prepared themselves. As a noted humorist observed, the most interesting thing about heavenly justice is that everyone will not get what they expect but exactly what they deserve.

Chapter 8

GRIEF AND
LONELINESS

Adam and Eve lived happily in the Garden of Eden, where they enjoyed the goodness that had been prepared for them. After a while they made choices that thrust them into mortality, where they learned about pleasure and pain, natural consequences of mortal life. God said to Eve, "I will greatly multiply thy sorrow and thy conception; in sorrow thou shalt bring forth children," and to Adam, He said, "Cursed is the ground for thy sake; in sorrow shalt thou eat of it all the days of thy life." (Genesis 3:16-17.)

Eve's joy and sorrow were both increased when she gained the capacity to procreate. Adam's lot was to till the stubborn earth, but his labors also fed him. These experiences of our first parents highlight the close connection between joy and sorrow, and their inevitability for all of us in this life. The process of becoming gods will give us experiences with grief that will build us up, even as they threaten to bring us to the ground.

The gospel of Jesus Christ can offer solace to us during times of grief if we activate our faith in Him. We can be certain that He knows and understands our pain because of His own earthly experiences. Isaiah was shown the Savior's suffering and described Him as "a man of sorrows, and acquainted with grief . . . Surely he hath borne our griefs, and carried our sorrows." (Isaiah 53:3-4.)

As we reflect on the life of Jesus, it becomes clear to us that He can empathize with our deepest feelings. We know that His sacrifices in Gethsamane and on Calvary transcended any suffering we will bear. He said, in a revelation given through the Prophet Joseph Smith, "I, God, have suffered these things for all, . . . which suffering caused myself, even God, the greatest of all, to tremble because of pain, and to bleed at every pore, and to suffer both body and spirit." (D&C 19:16-18.) In grief also, He has set the example for us.

Through revelation to the Saints in this day, the Lord has invited us to share our sorrow with Him: "If thou art sorrowful, call on the Lord thy God with supplication, that your souls may be joyful." (D&C 136:29.) Through prayer we can draw closer to Him and share our burdens.

The purpose of this life is to give us experiences necessary to grow into godhood. Sorrow and grief are natural occurrences here. We are a small but important part of a great, temporal existence characterized by change. On earth our spirits are also shrouded and limited in understanding by the veil of mortality. Caught, as we are, in the middle of life, it is easy for us to lose our eternal perspective and see things only as they relate to our earth life. We are saddened by death and rejoice at birth, but perhaps if a newborn's spirit were given a voice, he would tell us that he cries sometimes while grieving the world he is leaving.

This life is a series of beginnings and endings, some by choice and some by chance. At times we are jolted by the intensity of change or a heartbreaking loss, but most often, subtly and quietly, doors open and close. "Wow, what a grown-up boy you are," Aunt Katie says while stroking the hair of a four-year-old. His parents are startled to realize how quickly time has changed their toddler to a young boy. Yesterday they dressed and bathed him; today he can do it by himself.

Sadness and the Healing Process

Sadness is a natural occurrence in life and part of a healing process that takes place almost automatically. It would be inhuman not to respond with some emotion when faced with a loss or change. Sadness and depression that have been caused by a recognized event are often called "reactive depressions" by psychologists. At the completion of the grieving process, a shift back to more normal feelings takes place. We react to the stress in an appropriate and psychologically healthy manner. Sadness can turn destructive, however, if we refuse to let the healing take place, and depression can then become imbedded in our personality. A long period of grieving without a return to more normal moods is an indication that the natural process has been blocked.

Grieving is not frequently discussed, probably because the human instinct is to deny potential losses until they occur. Even when a loss appears inevitable, we tend to hold on to hope and pray for a miracle rather than beginning to cope through grieving. Though miracles do occur, more frequently the natural order of life rules and a loss is suffered. Grief is a universal human experience. It is as simple as saying good-bye and as wretched as the death of a spouse or sweetheart. It is the healing process that we pass through in reconstructing our spirit. Change, loss, and grief are parceled out at random among people, not equally nor according to personal righteousness. At times, huge losses spring up, threatening to entangle our feet and pull us to the ground; then the way becomes clear for a while.

Grieving is often sparked by changes in life and can occur even when there is not a clearly apparent loss. I remember lying in bed the first night after moving to a beautiful new home, exhausted from the move and feeling a little bit sad. I thought, "Maybe this feeling means

the move wasn't right for us. Maybe I made a mistake."
Then I recalled experiencing this very same feeling the
first night in the home we moved from, and the one before that, and when I traded in my old car, and when I
bought a stereo at age fourteen, and at other times of
change. One *constant* in the world is *change*. In the aftermath of changes, we juggle both the memory of the past
and the reality of the present. Because our minds,
bodies, and spirits do not always adapt as quickly as the
world transforms around us, the past and the present
are carried with us for a while with some confusion and
discomfort. It is during this period of adaptation, between the way things were and the way they are, that we
experience grief.

The Process of Grief

There is a natural pattern to grieving, whatever the
cause: first shock and denial, then anger and depression,
and finally, understanding and acceptance. Most people
think of grief as a process that takes months or years to
complete, such as the grief experienced at the death of a
child, a crippling disability, or a tragic accident. Grieving
may also take place in a few seconds; for instance, upon
finding a scratch in the door of your new car, or on dis-
covering that the brilliant yellow daffodils have withered
in the spring sun. The natural process of grieving takes
place in each of these instances. Grief is the time between
injury and renewal, however long it takes.

The initial reaction to loss or change is shock and denial, which can also be experienced as a general feeling
of numbness. Time seems to stop as we struggle to respond to the world. We feel unreal, as though we were
just watching the distant action around us. Our bodies
may feel heavy and tired, and we want to lie down and
sleep, hoping we will awaken to find that our loss was
only a dream. It is as if we were short-circuited and our
energy drained. We move in slow motion. The shock
sends us reeling into a frightening experience we would

never seek, but from which powerful lessons can be learned.

Anger and depression indicate that the second phase of grief has begun. We angrily search to find a reason for the misfortune and try to place blame on others or ourselves. Life also seems to have a certain sad and empty quality to it; something or someone is missing and is missed. Such depression is a natural response to change and the adaptations it demands. We long for things the way they were and are still uncertain about what is to come. The consequences of the loss or change become clearer as more normal routines return. Little things occur in day-to-day life that prompt memories: a song on the radio, driving through a certain part of town, or seeing an old photograph, for instance. The hurt experienced on these occasions is part of healing. Each time the loss is recalled and we are flooded with emotion, we grow, painfully at first, but more easily with the passage of time. Some days it seems as though there is too much to endure, and we slip back into despair; but another morning our burdens are slightly lighter, and we move on. Our strength waxes and wanes. We bruise easily and are vulnerable.

The final phase of grief is reconciliation—understanding and acceptance. We go on with life. We have not forgotten our loss, but because of it, we have taken a new direction. An understanding of what has happened to us may occur with time and the perspective it brings. There will be no explanations for many of us, though, except that we are human and live in an unpredictable, sometimes chaotic world. Waiting for understanding before we push ahead is not always possible. Life tugs at us again, sometimes playfully and sometimes poignantly, like an impatient child bidding for our attention. We need not be afraid; we can follow our instincts to join it again. Acceptance brings a release of the negative energy and ideas associated with grief. We recognize that persisting to carry them is only our burden and no consolation or tribute to our loss. The cycle of our life can then continue. We have grown from our experience and will love again.

Ann and Rick had known since October that they were having a baby, and from the first hint of their potential new arrival, their lives changed. Sales of baby clothes and furniture suddenly caught their attention, and the most popular topic of their late-night pillow talk became names for the baby. Preparing to be parents eclipsed any other activities. Even the Christmas holiday became pink and blue that year instead of the usual red and green; for Christmas, Ann received maternity clothes, and she gave Rick a wind-up baby swing. Then, in late winter Ann learned there was to be no baby. Later, with Rick at her side, the doctor confirmed that Ann had miscarried a few weeks earlier. "The products of conception will have to be removed surgically," he said in a matter-of-fact voice. They looked at each other, shocked and devastated. "This is our baby he's talking about. How can this be?"

That evening Rick and Ann sat in a hospital room and cried together, for their pain, for their dreams, and for their baby they had cherished and loved but would never see. Rick's sadness soon turned to anger. Why had this happened to him? He was keeping the commandments. He had always thought he would be a great father; he wanted it more than anything. Why had God chosen to hurt him in this way? He knew of plenty of folks who didn't want to have any more children, but they just kept coming. God could have kept this from happening; where was He? Rick faced this bitter disappointment without the comforting spirit of Christ because of his anger.

Rick passed quite quickly from the first stage of grief, shock and denial, to the second stage, anger and depression. He remained mired in anger for some time, blaming God and others for a natural (and heartbreaking) event in his life. Only after many months did he accept this personal tragedy. He was then able to grow spiritually and emotionally again.

Guilt and Unresolved Grief

Guilt can also paralyze us in the unresolved grief. The death or loss of a loved one prompts a searching of memories, and almost without fail, things are recalled that might have been said or done but were not. We long to turn back time, to have another chance and feel better about the separation. We dwell on those things left unsaid or undone, with our minds focused in the past; but looking backwards, we can't move safely forward. It is a rare and chance experience to be able to know the moment of passing so clearly that we can say a good-bye that leaves us feeling complete and satisfied. Perhaps it would be better to live in such a way that love is shown daily as much as possible.

Joan learned by a hurried phone call from her mother that her grandmother was dying. Joan and her grandmother had an especially loving relationship. During the past several years, the grandmother had been living with her family, and she and Joan had grown even closer. That morning the grandmother had gone to the doctor for a routine examination. While she was waiting in the office, she had a slight heart attack and was taken to a hospital, but en route she suffered a major attack and her heart stopped beating. The doctors quickly revived her and were in the process of installing a pacemaker when Joan was called by her mother. Joan was grief-stricken at the news. She thought about praying for a miraculous cure to spare her grandmother, but she unselfishly knelt and prayed that whatever happened, her grandmother would not suffer. A short time later her mother called again to say that the elderly woman had died. In spite of Joan's sadness, she felt peaceful and close to her. They had loved each other every day, and their love would reach beyond mortality and across time. That last day, she had prayed for God to meet her grandmother's needs rather than her own. Though it was not a perfect good-bye, Joan felt that her grandmother would continue her journey, sure of Joan's love.

Unresolved Grief

Though grieving is a natural process, it is possible to become stuck in one of its stages and experience even more intense hurt and pain than if we were to struggle to continue through it. Unresolved grief is a significant factor in the lives of many seriously depressed individuals even though they may not consciously realize it.

While Linda was traveling in Europe, her mother died suddenly in a hospital emergency room. The shock of her death left Linda afraid that she also would die of a broken heart or spirit. As she flew home to her family, she felt herself sliding into a deep, emotional crevice. Linda and her mother had supported each other through their blue moods in the past, and, at times, they had half-teased each other that one would not die without the other one. Linda believed that no one else could understand her or help her. "Who is there for me now?" she asked herself.

When she arrived home, Linda learned her mother had been seriously ill for a few days prior to her death but had not seen a doctor. She wondered why her father had not insisted that she seek help. Why had he waited until she was almost dead to take her to the hospital? Linda began to feel betrayed and suspicious. She was devastated by the death and angry that it hadn't been prevented. She thought her father was negligent and heartless and wondered if he had wanted her mother to die. Linda withdrew from her family and friends, refused to be comforted, and continued to look for signs of her father's malicious attitude toward her mother. She found that living in her father's home brought back too many haunting memories, so she moved out and cut off contact with her family. Everything seemed to remind her of the loss of her mother, and she desperately searched for someone or something to take away her pain. Though Linda felt almost normal for short periods of time, depression would always return, especially around holidays or anniversaries. She began to think about suicide as a way to be with her mother again.

Normal grief had turned into serious depression because Linda focused so much energy on remaining angry and on blocking attempts by others to comfort her. She encouraged depression by continually stirring the embers of her grief until they would erupt in flames, often fueled by her bitter feelings about her father.

In the midst of a deep depression, Linda asked for professional help. She said at the outset of treatment that her mother's death was no longer an issue. While relating her story, though, her tears indicated she still had some healing left to do. Linda had been frozen in place the day her mother died; shock and devastation had not been replaced by other phases of the healing process. Reconciliation or other attempts to go on with life somehow seemed to indicate disloyalty to the memory of her mother. Heartbreak and anger were all she allowed herself to feel. Her first steps toward recovery were painful too. One day as Linda closed her eyes and imagined her mother's face, the therapist asked, "How would your mother want you to be feeling?" Tears gently slid down her cheeks as she said, "She'd want me to be happy, to feel close to my family and have good friends I could talk with." Linda realized that grief was carrying her away from her mother's dreams and wishes. Bitterness and sorrow were not a fitting legacy to her memory.

No one whom we have loved would want us to spend our lives grieving about them. We can expect to be taken to the depths of sadness by the death of a loved one, but we do a disservice to that person's hope for our success and happiness by locking ourselves away. Vowing never to love again because we have lost our love is shortsighted and somewhat selfish. A much better tribute is to share with others the new appreciation for love and life that has grown within us.

My little boy was despondent when his kitten suddenly died. They had been very close; they played to their mutual delight every day and slept side by side every night. A tearful little boy buried his friend one spring morning with his equally touched mother offering comfort. For days he would see Muffin's toys and cry a little, or call for his kitty, forgetting for an instant that he was gone. His mother suggested another cat, but how could he love one as much as Muffin? A few weeks passed and the hurt began to heal. One day he came through the door with a new kitten a playmate had found on the schoolyard the day before. It was tiny, scrawny, and unkempt, but somehow the kitten's need for love transcended my son's loyalty to the memory of his friend. His grieving completed, he could love again.

God does not want us to grieve forever. As doors are closed by change, loss, or the passing of loved ones, we experience an opportunity to grow. My son learned about love and compassion through the death of his kitten. No one would have wished for or actively sought this experience, but his life was enriched by it. So it is with us. Since Adam and Eve, loss and change have been an intricate part of the human struggle and essential in our schooling to become gods. The challenge is to take our measure of sorrow, to know the pangs of the spirit it can bring, and to grow, refusing to become embittered and spiritually stunted. Perhaps grief is, most of all, an experience of the spirit.

Loneliness

Grief and loneliness often occur simultaneously, sparked by the same change or loss. At other times we may suddenly feel lonely for no apparent reason. Perhaps it was these occasions that Eliza R. Snow alluded to in her song "O My Father" when she wrote, "Yet ofttimes a secret something whispered, 'You're a stranger here.' " Loneliness is a certain sad feeling that is common to us all.

People who suffer from loneliness often believe that their feelings are unique and indicative of some great failure within themselves. The truth is that everyone feels lonely from time to time, whether single or married, shy or gregarious, beautiful or plain. Loneliness is more than just being alone. Many people actively seek the chance to spend hours or days by themselves collecting their thoughts, making decisions, or just relaxing, and do not feel lonely. The depressing side of loneliness is negative feelings, such as despair and self-loathing, created by thoughts such as these: "If I were more handsome I would have real friends," or "I'm so dumb, nobody wants to talk to me." Loneliness can, at other times, be a positive signal too. It can let us know when it is time to reach outside ourselves for new friends and opportunities or to strengthen our existing relationships.

Just as loneliness is more than being alone, so happiness is more than being with someone else. Really satisfying relationships take time to build and a lot of nurturing. But even in relationships of substance, there are times when we must be alone.

Loneliness does not equal unattractiveness, and being alone is not a signal that we are unworthy of anyone. Believing either of these ideas can lead to desperation, which is particularly unattractive to people who are happy with themselves, the kind of friends we want to cultivate.

Scriptures have been cited occasionally in a manner that reinforces negative thinking about being alone, such as Genesis 2:18: "God said, It is not good that the man should be alone." Taken out of context, we might suppose that the life of single people was being condemned here, and, unfortunately, some have compromised important values to avoid being alone, believing that their failure to seek a mate in this life would lead to eternal condemnation. Clearly the scripture refers to

Adam's particular need for Eve in order to fulfill his earthly purpose. Being alone certainly does not break commandments or indicate unrighteousness. The Bible records that Christ often sought time to be alone, to pray and reflect on His ministry.

Being a single adult in the Church is not as uncommon as many people believe. Many good brothers and sisters have chosen not to remarry following the death of their mates, and many others have not felt impressed to marry for various personal reasons. We do not condemn them for making these choices, but are often not as kind in our self-judgments. These critical thoughts promote feelings that are more demoralizing and depressing than motivating.

Existential philosophers teach that the recognition that we are *all* actually alone is both a great crisis and a great opportunity for growth in life: a crisis because the natural inclination of man seems to be toward depending on others, and an opportunity for growth because following the realization that we are alone, we can then shape life according to higher principles than seeking the approval of others.

The title of a recent bestseller is *Being Your Own Best Friend,* good advice in any situation, but particularly salient during times of depression and loneliness. We can't wait for happiness until someone comes along who we believe can make us happy. This is the "Sleeping Beauty" fantasy; we wait passively to be discovered by our "handsome prince" (never thinking that we might have to kiss a few toads along the way!). Unfortunately, the kinds of people we want to be close to are looking for relationships with active, lively, and vibrant people, not for people who are desperately seeking to meet their own needs. Now is the time for each of us to prepare to feel close to someone by learning how to meet our own needs and becoming sensitive to ourselves. Being alone doesn't have to mean that we are unhappy, though we can certainly arrange it that way. We can each become our own best friend by doing things that we enjoy and treating ourselves well. We can treat ourselves now as we would like others to treat us.

Perhaps the most important thing to realize about loneliness is that it is often brief and transitory. Though some individuals feel unattached and lonely for most of their lives, this is relatively rare. It is unrealistic, however, to expect to escape all feelings of loneliness, whether we are alone or with other people. Here are a few suggestions for overcoming these occasional feelings and fears:

1. *Concentrate on successful relationships.* Some individuals refuse to use their friends for comfort or solace when they are blue. They search futilely for someone new to take their lonely feelings away. Usually, however, when people are feeling down, their capacity to form new relationships is low, and this leads to more desperate feelings of loneliness and frustration. Strive to cultivate and appreciate the friends you already have.

2. *Focus on quality, not quantity.* Research has indicated that a person with one close and intimate friend is less apt to develop serious episodes of long-term depression than someone who has several "acquaintances." There is apparently psychological benefit in nurturing deep, lasting relationships. Some individuals have a pattern of collecting friends and admirers without taking the time to cultivate deeper feelings. They seem to hope that quantity can substitute for their lack of willingness or ability to commit to real intimacy. This need for more and more friends to help one escape loneliness becomes like a bottomless pit, and it is impossible to fill it with superficial relationships.

3. *Be realistic.* No one will totally escape experiencing feelings of loneliness from time to time. Let us learn to accept them as natural and sometimes helpful signals about where we are in life.

4. *Spend quality time alone.* We can use time alone as Jesus did, for personal reflection and growth or to be-

come involved in satisfying and pleasant activities. It is doubtful that anyone comes to value being alone if he only engages in self-criticism or distasteful activities. A handy way to measure this is to ask ourselves, "Would I choose to be sharing this activity with someone else?" If the answer is no, perhaps we are making ourselves miserable and reinforcing the notion that being alone is unsatisfying and boring.

Loneliness need not be overwhelming if we keep a realistic perspective about feeling lonely, cultivate the skill of enjoying time alone, and build relationships that can offer comfort and support.

Chapter 9

COPING WITH ANGER

Since the days of Sigmund Freud, some psychological theories have promoted the idea that anger is a forerunner of depression. These theories speculate that unexpressed, pent-up anger and frustration are ultimately turned against oneself because they are not dealt with in more appropriate ways. Suicide attempts and other self-destructive behaviors are viewed as linked to an individual's anger at himself or others.

As a result of these theories, a number of therapies have developed that advocate open expression of anger by direct confrontation, catharsis (yelling, screaming, crying, or talking it out), by acting out the anger through hitting safe objects or taking it out by aggressive activity, as in sports. None of these methods has been particularly successful, however, perhaps because they focus more on what to do with anger than how to avoid getting boiling mad. In fact, it has also been learned that involvement in some aggressive types of activities that were formerly advocated as therapeutic actually decreases the control one may have over coping with anger.

Some individuals believe that anger just *is*, and nothing can be done about it. Folklore supports this naive attitude by teaching that redheads are more easily angered than blonds or brunettes and even that whole ethnic groups are naturally "hot tempered." While there is some scientific evidence that certain kinds of illnesses, brain damage, or early childhood experiences may cause a person to suffer from a lower threshold of anger, these categories include only a small percentage of the population. Early modeling of patterns of violence or anger can also predispose one to experience increased anger as an adult and to respond more readily with aggression. These influences on behavior are so powerful that many abused children become abusive adults; such types of problems indicate a need to consult with a counselor. For most people, however, anger is an emotion they can learn to control.

The primary key for taking control over anger is contained in the expression "The more I thought about it, the angrier I became!" In a talk delivered in the Salt Lake Tabernacle in 1853, Brigham Young demonstrated insight into the connection between thoughts and anger when he counseled, "Suppose, when you arrive at home from this meeting, you find your neighbors have killed your horses and destroyed your property, how would you feel? You would feel like taking instant vengeance on the perpetrator of the deed. But it would be wrong for you to encourage the least particle of feeling to arise like anger, or revenge, or like taking judgment into your own hands, until the Lord Almighty shall say, 'Judgment is yours, and for you to execute.' . . . When anger arises, . . . know that it arises in yourselves." (*Journal of Discourses* 2:134-35). President Young was correct: the root of anger is within us, and we can control its expression as well as decrease its effect on us.

Anger, like any emotion, is triggered by thoughts. For instance, in a basketball game if a player catches an occasional elbow in the ribs by a teammate, he usually attributes it to aggressive hustling. If, however, he is elbowed repeatedly by a member of the opposing team, he becomes angry. The pain is the same, but the meaning the player attributes to the action is different. When we become angry, it is because our thoughts tell us we should do so. The meaning we assign to words, actions, or intentions causes our anger. Because of the relationship between thoughts and feelings, no one can *make* us angry if we don't allow them to.

Why Anger?

Anger is just one emotion of many that human beings experience. Some people, however, are able to respond only with anger to events that appear to have negative consequences. This emotional pattern occurs almost like a physical reflex; without thinking, the person reacts automatically in what seems to be a natural manner. Though few people are naturally angry, many have trained themselves to respond this way because it has been superficially advantageous.

Some individuals claim that they can use angry thoughts to motivate themselves to action. This may occasionally be true, but more often anger promotes distorted thinking, depression, and decreased energy. Initially, as they plan their strategy to get even, they may mistakenly label their obsessive thoughts, inability to fall asleep, or early morning awakening as an increase in their energy level. Soon, however, motivation fades, negative thinking increases, and depression ensues.

Movies often depict so-called heroes who are wronged by others, become intensely angry, and develop creative ways to bring about justice and take revenge on their enemies. These fantasies grossly misrepresent how anger affects people because in reality it limits creative thought and productive problem-solving and replaces them with obsessive, one-track thinking and distorted ideas. The image of the angry person "seeing red" and losing control is much more accurate than that of the Hollywood hero who gets mad and reestablishes truth and justice.

People have begun to claim a *right* to be angry, and in a sense, they are correct. We do have a right to assert ourselves and ask for fair treatment, but just becoming angry seldom accomplishes anything. In fact, it often leads to negative consequences, such as high blood pressure from increased tension, strained relationships, and low self-esteem. Ultimately, anger can lead to depression.

There are few long-term advantages for responding with anger. It is most often an emotional attempt to get our way, to intimidate people, or to make our rules apply to others. If it works, we experience a false sense of personal power, but when it fails, we lose self-esteem and risk depression.

Learning Patterns of Anger

Some anger-centered styles of relating with others begin in early childhood. For example, while at the grocery store with his father, three-year-old Jason asks for some candy. Dad says no, but Jason takes a candy bar and begins to unwrap it anyway. When his father takes the candy away and returns it to the shelf, he begins to cry loudly and refuses to go on shopping. Reluctantly, but predictably, his father gives in to Jason's wish in order to avoid a scene. What Jason's father does not realize is that he might have avoided a scene in the store, but he has reinforced a pattern of tantrums and helped to create a spoiled boy, teenager, and adult who will continue to throw a tantrum to get his way the rest of his life. From this experience, and others like it, Jason learns that he can manipulate others in order to get his way by becoming angry and begins to use his anger to control people.

Expressing anger uncontrollably is another adult form of throwing a tantrum. Some misinformed people believe that really telling someone off and yelling are the most helpful alternatives to dealing with their feelings. Hours and days are then spent brooding about their

unhappiness or injury, planning what they will say or re-
hashing what they said. These negative thoughts, however,
make them feel more miserable than their tongue-lashing
caused the object of their anger to feel. Improper or extreme responses to other people and situations generally
increase during this period of angry ruminations, and
even minor incidents can provoke torrents of misdirected
rage. Violence is not uncommon among people who allow
their simmering, angry thoughts to rule them. Perhaps
this vulnerability to overreact, which people experience
when they are burdened with anger, could be a reason
why Christ counseled that anger can put one in danger
of the judgment. (See Matthew 5:21-22.)

Anger is also frequently at the core of very destructive patterns in relationships between adults. It destroys
intimacy and trust, which are essential for closeness. One
expects, as intimacy develops and long periods are spent
together, that each partner will come to know the other
person's frailties and weak spots. This vulnerability is
natural, healthy, and promotes even greater closeness if
each partner continues to feel loved. When a couple
begin to point to or complain about their partner's faults
during episodes of anger, however, they erode the trust
that is necessary to sustain the relationship. Many
couples who seek marital therapy have fallen prey to this
pattern of arguments or disagreements that lead to personal criticism, and for some, their wounds have become
too deep to heal.

Dean and Mitzi had been married about twenty years
when they entered counseling. They were both intelligent, but they had developed the habit of using their
sharp minds to focus on the weaknesses of others.
Whenever Dean or Mitzi became frustrated, angry, or
hurt, they unleashed a torrent of criticism (which they
called "zingers") on each other. They naively hoped
their words would help them to "get even" and recover
the self-esteem they thought had been lost. Criticism,
however, only prompted the partner to respond in a

similar manner. Since neither Dean nor Mitzi was willing to ignore the provocation of the other, before long a small grievance could be escalated into a marital disaster. They also feared being devastated if they didn't try to retaliate. The result of these battles was inevitably destructive to both of them, no matter who got in the last zinger, because in the aftermath, what they each remembered about the fight was the biting comments made about *them*, and they carried this pain with them until their next fight.

Angry and critical comments lead to defensiveness and futile attempts to regain the upper hand. The problems escalate as both partners become increasingly defensive and begin to counterattack. Even if one could win the argument, he must sacrifice so much self-esteem in the process that it is hardly worth the price. Mitzi and Dean discovered that the wounds of emotional warfare were slow to heal, even with apologies, good intentions, and progress in altering this pattern. This couple, and others with similar problems, remain like shell-shocked soldiers, hypersensitive and prone to overreact to any marital stress.

Assertiveness Versus Anger

Consistent failure to act assertively can also increase the risk that patterns of anger and depression will develop. A nonassertive approach to life may be chosen for a number of reasons: the fear of arousing an angry response from someone else, fear of rejection or retaliation if one states his opinion, unrealistic expectations that others will anticipate and meet one's needs, or the false belief that one has no rights and must accept less than his fair share because of societal rules. Regardless of the cause, nonassertive people are also prone to anger, and at times this anger leads to depression.

Women are particularly susceptible to anger generated by a nonassertive style. Former traditions tightly defined the roles and behavior of women in society and thereby limited the acceptability of women expressing themselves openly. Some women who have not dared question these societal *shoulds* are unaware of their anger because it has been covered for years with layers of depression. Successful treatment of their depression must include recognition of their angry feelings, coping with them, and then letting them go.

It is important to remember that assertiveness is not demonstrated through aggressiveness. Assertiveness is standing up for your rights and asking for a fair share in a direct manner. An assertive person respects the rights and individuality of others and expects the same kind of respect in return.

Black, White, and Seeing Red

It is common and somewhat comforting for people to place events and people in categories at extreme opposites of each other and thereby simplify the world into black and white, as in an old-time western movie where the good guys try to win out over the bad guys. This tendency is increased even further when people become upset and angry. Unrealistically viewing detractors as all bad or exaggerating their bad intentions provides more justification for negative feelings and causes them to escalate. Studies of racially motivated lynchings and other violent activities have documented that by exaggerating complaints and attributing inhuman qualities to victims, leaders of mobs can incite ordinary people to commit actions that they normally abhor. The early history of The Church of Jesus Christ of Latter-day Saints contains many examples of persecution that developed in this fashion. Jesus attempted to deter this process and break down "them versus us" attitudes when He taught, "Ye hath heard that it hath been said, Thou shalt love thy neighbour, and hate thine enemy. But I say unto you, Love your enemies, bless them that curse you, do good to them that hate you, and pray for them which despitefully use you, and persecute you; that ye may be the children of your Father which is in heaven; for he maketh his sun to rise on the evil and on the good, and sendeth rain on the just and on the unjust." (Matthew 5:43-45.) Jesus knew that even the most evil among us is not *all* bad, and He has asked us to leave judgment to God.

Loving our enemies increases our ability to see their good points because it forces us to stop thinking negatively about them and to strive in their behalf, if only in prayer. This change in attitude causes discomfort or dissonance within us, which is usually resolved by our admission that we had formerly held a tainted and false opinion of them. It is by obedience to these commandments that we can gain a more realistic perspective on the world, greater control over anger, and more peace in our hearts. Jesus taught that there are no benefits to be gained by maintaining grudges, staging reprisals, or holding onto anger in any form.

Though Christ's charge to love our enemies may seem like a sign of weakness to some, it is actually a formula for replacing the inner strength lost in anger. Holding on to anger places us in a vulnerable and weak position; the ability to think and act rationally is diminished and our self-esteem is continually under attack by negative memories of what provoked the anger. To the Ephesians Paul wrote, "Can ye be angry, and not sin? . . . Let all bitterness, and wrath, and anger, and clamour, and evil speaking, be put away from you, with all malice; and be ye kind one to another, tenderhearted, forgiving one another." (Joseph Smith Translation, Ephesians 4:26, 31-32.) When we remain angry, not only are we in danger of acting sinfully toward the object of our anger, but we are also weakened and less able to resist lashing out at others.

Self-esteem and Anger

Low self-esteem contributes to a low threshold for experiencing and expressing feelings of anger. When people believe they have no value and nothing to contribute, they frequently become hypersensitive to the comments and actions of others, fearing that others will also criticize their faults. Unfortunately, their ability to discern what is being said or done is impaired by low self-esteem, and they frequently misunderstand others. Anger and defensiveness result because they feel criticized and attacked in many innocuous situations. Individuals who have a poor self-image may also express anger or criticize others in a futile attempt to feel that they are not the only ones who are not perfect.

A healthy level of self-esteem is necessary to modulate all emotions, especially anger. It acts like a filter on information we receive from the world, allowing comments or actions that are not consistent with our self-image to pass from our minds without undo worry. Without this filter, we may take many things people say or do seriously and become angry and hurt. Self-esteem also enhances our sense of humor, which is characteristically lacking in most angry people.

Righteous Anger

Christ's clearing of the temple in Jerusalem is an example of righteous anger, anger that is expressed for a positive purpose and in a useful, appropriate manner. Few people are able to distinguish what made this occasion unique from their everyday anger, however, and become confused about how and when to use it. Perhaps another look at this incident can clarify the principles involved in the righteous use of anger.

Jesus had visited the temple many times and understood its purpose and importance. He had observed the moneychangers and merchants there, knew their manner of business, which included dishonesty with others and perversion of the laws of offerings and sacrifice, and had doubtless tried to teach them the true principles of temple worship. At Passover, "Jesus went into the temple, and began to cast out them that sold and bought in the temple, and overthrew the tables of the moneychangers, and the seats of them that sold doves; and would not suffer that any man should carry any vessel through the temple. And he taught, saying unto them, Is it not written, My house shall be called of all nations the house of prayer? but ye have made it a den of thieves." (Mark 11:15-17.)

Jesus, with the authority of his Father and a complete understanding of the situation in the temple, drove out those who were desecrating it. He did not seek revenge by harming them or destroying their merchandise, and He did not call them names, lecture them at length, or repeatedly attack their character. After removing the merchants and moneychangers, He briefly tried to teach them the sacred purpose of the temple so that they might make better choices in the future.

In a revelation given through Joseph Smith, Jesus repeated these principles of the righteous use of anger: "Reproving betimes with sharpness, when moved upon by the Holy Ghost; and then showing forth afterwards an increase of love toward him whom thou has reproved, lest he esteem thee to be his enemy." (Doctrine and Covenants 121:43-44.) Two difficult challenges are included in this commandment: using spiritual promptings to determine when to express anger, and immediately showing love to someone after we have reproved them. Anger can be useful only when it is expressed in a manner that allows constructive change to take place, and we are instructed to let that be a spiritual decision. If we act offensively or with malice, however, those whom we are trying to reach will turn away. They must be reminded with a show of love that our expressions of anger are made out of genuine concern for them.

Letting Go of Anger

Just experiencing angry thoughts and feelings is not necessarily a good reason to express them. Emotions are constantly with us—love, caring, sadness, or elation, for example—but are not frequently expressed. Some well-meaning people focus their attention on letting anger out whenever it is experienced, but except for a few cases, this does not prove useful. The truth is that just *expressing* anger does not, by itself, offer relief. It is actually *letting go* of the angry thoughts that allows healing to occur.

The benefits of expressing anger can be weighed by answering two questions: Is my anger appropriate and useful? Will it benefit me or others to express it?

We need to determine first if anger is an appropriate and useful response. This is done by checking out our understanding of what has been said or done. Communication problems, such as misunderstandings and false interpretations, are common causes of angry feelings. Because anger arises so suddenly, we too often trust our first feelings, assume we have been intentionally slighted, and refuse to try to clarify the situation. It is easy and normal to misunderstand the intentions of others from time to time. Investigating what was really meant is valuable because it delays a hasty and, perhaps, inappropriate response and allows for constructive communication instead of anger. We should also consider the usefulness of expressing anger. It will likely arouse defensiveness, limit constructive communication, and decrease our ability to problem solve. If expressing ourselves just leads to an escalation of bad feelings, we have accomplished little.

There are, of course, some possible benefits of recognizing and expressing anger. Angry feelings are a signal that something is not right; perhaps it is something about us, the situation, or the message we have just heard. Each of these variables, or a combination of them, has the power to produce anger. When expressed constructively, anger is also an important sign to others that our feelings count. Anger ceases to be beneficial, however, when it is out of control, when it is used to attack others or motivates a person to seek revenge. In each of these circumstances, the angry person goes beyond a reasonable statement of his feelings and tries to impose his will or judgment on another.

Anger frequently is more harmful to the one experiencing it than to the one at whom it is directed. Holding onto anger makes us tense, edgy, and more easily frustrated. It is extremely stressful physically, mentally, emotionally, and spiritually and takes its toll on us in a myriad of ways. If someone is genuinely out to harm us, we greatly assist them by remaining angry. If we are angry, we can ask ourselves, Is this helpful to me or is it an additional hurt?

How to Control Anger

Take time out.

There is much folk wisdom about getting control of anger, and some of it, such as counting to ten or taking the anger out on an inanimate object, is not bad. These two suggestions give us time away from the cause of anger and provide a chance to let it subside or to develop constructive alternatives. There are usually better ways to deal with difficult situations that occur to us when we are caught in a heated confrontation. Walking away from these situations is an indication of inner strength and is just good sense.

Just leaving the scene does not always solve the problem, however. It is not uncommon for people to continue to ruminate about a provocative event for some time after it occurs; anger can ruin our whole day, or even longer. The habit of holding on to anger invites depression because it inevitably includes negative thoughts and reduced self-esteem. Animals have a much better system for dealing with anger; after a fight or a scolding, they lie down to rest and forget it. Because of this strategy, they are probably much happier and healthier than humans. Have you ever heard of a dog who died of high blood pressure?

Replace negative thoughts with positive ones.

Stopping and diverting negative, angry thoughts are

other ways we can cope productively with lingering feelings. Thoughts can be stopped by saying no verbally and shaking our head, wearing a rubber band on our wrist and flipping it when an unwanted idea occurs, switching to a preplanned positive thought immediately as a replacement for a negative one, or in several other ways that were introduced in chapter 1.

Whenever a thought is removed, it is important to put a positive thought in its place immediately to keep it from recurring. We might select two or three positive past or future events and practice automatically diverting our thoughts to them, imagining these events in as much detail as possible. The more we put in it, the more powerful this tool becomes. Thoughts can also be diverted to poetry, scriptures, songs, or landscapes; anything that is uplifting and can be committed to memory can be used. Redecorating our minds with pleasant and happy thoughts will free us of destructive anger.

Recognize that others have different values.

Shoulds can play an important role in the development of anger when we naively expect others to follow our rules and ideas about what constitutes acceptable behavior. Most behavior and many values are relative to the situation. If we took off our shoes before entering a home, for example, or carried our groceries home from market in a basket on our heads, or honked our horn each time we entered an intersection, most people would think we were acting in a rather bizarre manner, yet these are common practices in other parts of the world. Similarly, we are incorrect if we believe that our particular sets of rules about life and how to interact with others are shared by everyone else. It is immature to become angry simply because our rules are not followed or our needs are not met.

The old Indian axiom of withholding judgment of someone until we have "walked in their moccasins" provides another strategy to control angry feelings through empathy. Carlos, a group-therapy patient, became livid because his doctor had not greeted him in the waiting room prior to the group session, though the doctor had walked into the room to take another patient back for her appointment. For almost one-half of the group, Carlos villified doctors and other professionals as unfeeling, uncaring, and pompous idiots. If he had observed this particular doctor during a day, however, he would have understood that focusing only on the patient he was seeing at that moment was part of his style. Even his co-worker's greetings were often ignored as he went about his tasks. Carlos's *should* about always greeting those you know was a custom foreign to his doctor's world.

Developing the ability to empathize with others can decrease anger dramatically. Carlos would have been much happier if he had tried to understand his doctor's behavior instead of assuming it was directed at him. Letting go of the idea that our *shoulds* apply to everyone else is the first step in utilizing the power of empathy. Next we must try to understand the other person's motivation in order to put the interaction with them in a more realistic perspective. Finally, decisions about what to do with our angry feelings can be made based on the two questions presented earlier: Is my anger appropriate and useful? Will it benefit me or others to express it?

Change behavior through positive shaping rather than anger.

We are able to effect greater change through positive shaping of behavior than through anger. There are a few exceptions to this rule, such as when a child has placed himself in danger by disobeying directions, and quick, strong, and memorable actions must be taken. Only when an immediate, simple point must be made in an intense manner is punishment more useful than praise, however. Angry or punitive actions undermine healthy relationships, create defensiveness, and generate negative feelings in those whom they are directed toward. Instead of pointing out behaviors that make us unhappy, we can praise and reward those actions which bring us joy. This simple formula is especially useful in long-term relationships, such as marriages, that have become strained. Focusing on what's right promotes feelings of hope and provides relief from confrontation and anger.

Let go of angry feelings.

Paul wrote to the Ephesians, "Let not the sun go down upon your wrath" (Ephesians 4:26), apparently to encourage them to deal with as much anger as they could during the day and let go of the rest. There are some things we can do to cope with angry feelings, but it is fruitless and even destructive to hold onto those feelings if nothing further can be done. A modern derivation of this rule frequently repeated as advice to married couples is "Never go to bed angry." Not all problems can be resolved in one day, of course, but making an effort to let go of those things that we cannot change will increase our sense of inner peace.

Take time to prevent misunderstandings.

It is impossible to consistently understand what others mean by their words or behavior, and taking the time to check out our interpretations of their actions can prevent a lot of unnecessary anger. This strategy offers the advantages of (1) a buffer of time between the perceived hurt and the response, (2) allowing us to clarify what we have heard, and (3) giving others a chance to consider if they have given the message they intended to give. Many people resist this method of controlling anger because they feel it is silly or they want to place the responsibility for clear communication on others. Since it is impossible for anyone to be perfectly in touch at all times with his surroundings and able to understand fully what is taking place, it is irresponsible not to take the time to check it out.

Learn to use disarming techniques to deal with criticism.

Sometimes it is necessary to deal with the anger of others when we feel that it is unjustified (just because someone is angry, it doesn't mean that they are correct, of course). In his book *Feeling Good,* Dr. David Burns provides a practical method for managing these situations with a tool he calls the "disarming technique." First, he advocates finding a grain of truth or a way to agree in principle with part of what the other person says. This will allow us to respond in a way that lets the other person know that his criticism has been heard. It is important to avoid fighting back or using sarcasm, because that will only make the situation worse, causing everyone's feelings to escalate and become uncontrollable. After we have acknowledged the other person's dissatisfaction, we should restate our position in a clear and unaggressive manner. It may take a few interactions for our accuser to realize that he has been heard *and* we do not agree, but he will feel that his opinion has at least been respected, and we will avoid a destructive argument.

It is sometimes very difficult to put this technique to work; our emotions and old patterns of behavior get the best of us, and we slip back into our former habits of confrontation and defensiveness. We can practice using the disarming technique by role-playing with a friend or mentally rehearsing the steps until they are committed to memory. Being prepared in advance to manage criticism will decrease the chances of our becoming angry and hurting ourselves further.

Allow others free agency.

It is difficult to let people we love make choices we don't agree with or that we see as destructive, particularly in a family. As children become teenagers and adults try to direct or change them, too much criticism can lead to anger and resentment. Developing the courage and skill to say "It's his choice" and then letting go of our wishes to change others can help us avoid unnecessary and unproductive worry and hurt feelings.

Anger does take time and practice to control. Because it has become a habitual response in some situations, it must be removed and replaced with other ways of responding. Unfortunately, however, the times we get angry are the times when it is hardest to think rationally and gain control; in initiating new responses that are as powerful as old habits, we must use a lot of advanced preparation and creativity.

James placed the ultimate results of anger in perspective when he wrote, "Let every man be swift to hear, slow to speak, slow to wrath: for the wrath of man worketh not the righteousness of God." (James 1:19-20.) Controlling anger brings us closer to godliness and blocks a possible entry route of depression.

Chapter 10

HELPING
OTHERS

 The Church of Jesus Christ
of Latter-day Saints has often been recognized for its efforts in reaching out to help in times of need, not only to
its members, but also to others who have experienced
misfortune. During disasters such as the famine in Africa,
the floods in Utah and Idaho, and earthquakes in Latin
America, the Church has provided needed food, medi-
cine, clothing, and shelter to victims as well as structure
to organize the Saints and others in relief efforts. This
willingness to give assistance and support both as an organization and as individuals is a hallmark of true Christianity.

 For each of us, there are also personal crises and disasters during which our burdens can be lightened by
the compassionate service of others and, at times, by the
giving of ourselves. Depressed individuals in particular
are helped both by the love they receive and by the care
they give to others. Since depression is a time when questions about our self-worth and value are endless, the concern shown by others is a reminder that we do matter.
Through providing service to people in need, we can
also escape, even for a few minutes, from the narrow and

negative feelings of depression and, in doing so, help to rebuild self-esteem.

The Art of the Helper

Helping people through periods of depression is an art, because the helper must constantly struggle to maintain a sense of balance about his efforts. It is often difficult and frustrating to try to reach out to those who are depressed. They often seem pessimistic and uncertain about suggestions, and they challenge, deflect, and reject attempts of others to build their feelings of self-esteem. Because they feel so hopeless, they may refuse to listen at all. Sometimes it is hard not to feel personally rejected by them.

Progress for those who are depressed can be slow and unpredictable. The patterns that cause depression become so automatic that the person affected cannot experience change without making consistent and strenuous efforts. Recovery is rocky. Even under the best of conditions, there are inevitable setbacks and regressions. Those who are trying to be of assistance, even the professionals, often feel frustrated by the apparent lack of progress.

The most important role of the helper is to offer sincere and consistent understanding, encouragement, and support. The ability to listen and understand is a critical skill, and the ability to do this well will, in large measure, determine how helpful the helper will be.

Depressed individuals often feel isolated because of their belief that no one understands them. In order to demonstrate understanding and gain their confidence, it is essential to listen patiently to their story. Sometimes even offering them this much care can make a big difference and boost their self-esteem, since they have often come to expect being cut off or avoided by others.

Many well-meaning helpers mistakenly try to minimize the sadness or loneliness the depressed person feels because they believe that this will change his perspective and improve his mood. This intervention is seldom effective because it alienates the person they are trying to help. Since most people open up to others a little at a time, the helper must initially understand what the other person is experiencing and avoid making hasty judgments or trying to talk him out of his problem, since this only discourages further sharing and decreases his trust in the helper. Try to gain a clear understanding of "where it hurts" before you begin to offer suggestions.

It is important to keep in mind that each person experiences different facets of depression. Listen carefully in order to understand how it is affecting the person you are trying to help. The tendency to stereotype people and lump them together in broad categories leads people to assume that they know all about depression if they have known someone who overcame it, or if they have had personal experience with it themselves. Though there are general similarities, each person's experience is unique and requires a little different kind of help and encouragement. Ignoring these differences makes a helper seem insensitive and unskilled.

Be honest about the seriousness of the problem and the efforts necessary for change. Since patterns of depression usually develop over a long period of time, they often require some time to resolve, and a number of interventions may need to be tried before the person starts to feel better. For some people, a medical doctor may need to be consulted to evaluate potential medical concerns, or a psychologist may be needed for psychotherapy. Honesty helps create the trust that is necessary to be a successful helper.

Facilitating Change

It is difficult to know when someone is ready to experiment with changes in his life. A common problem that helpers experience is wanting to offer a lot of specific advice and suggestions before the other person is able to use them, which usually leads to frustration and sometimes disillusionment and rejection. If you choose to give advice, the best tactic is to begin with small steps and quicken the pace only after experiencing some successes. Monitor carefully what is actually *done,* as well as what is said. Actions are usually a truer measure of ability to change than are words.

A frequent result of offering advice before the person is ready to change is described in the psychological game that Eric Berne calls "Why don't you . . . Yes, but . . ." In this type of interaction, one person appears to be soliciting advice from another, who obliges, only to discover that the suggestions are dismissed in a wave of excuses and qualifications. This is very demoralizing for both people. The would-be helper feels frustrated because the advice was ignored, and the depressed person interprets it as reinforcement for his feeling that he is hopeless and nothing can be done. The best way to escape this destructive game is to refuse to play. If the person you are trying to assist doesn't seem to be willing to try even the smallest of your suggestions, he is probably not ready for the kind of help you can offer. Talk with him about this concern in a direct and caring manner.

Avoid offering simplistic remedies or advocating drastic changes to depressed individuals. Though they may seem to be pleading for a quick and easy cure, these are rarely successful. Oversimplifying the problem makes people feel misunderstood and the would-be helper seem superficial and naive. Offering suggestions for quick changes usually undermines the helper's credibility because the suggestions don't work, and even if they did, most people are unlikely to follow through with them.

Encourage involvement in pleasurable activities to help decrease depression. Though this is often the fastest way to improve mood, it is also one of the hardest to accomplish. If you know what the person has enjoyed in the past, get involved with him in these kinds of activities. If possible, it is usually better to participate with the person than to just make suggestions, because depressed individuals often lack the motivation to organize activities for themselves. Don't be afraid to enjoy yourself when you're together. Pleasure, like laughter, can be contagious. Providing a model of happiness or satisfaction, while still respecting the person's feelings, can help lift his spirits.

Most people excel at something, but they often neglect their positive achievements when they are depressed. Encourage those who are depressed in things they are likely to do successfully in order to rebuild self-confidence. Remember that achieving success in a few small things is better than tackling a large project that does not provide quick, positive feedback.

Obstacles to Change

A number of tactics that people use when trying to help others are destructive to their relationships and unlikely to facilitate positive changes. Most of these are based on some kind of punishment if the person fails to meet the expectation of the helper.

Making threats or delivering ultimatums is almost always counterproductive. Some people mistakenly believe that if they can just say or do something dramatic to "shake them out of it," depression can be relieved. Unfortunately, these strategies usually increase depression, since the person cannot comply and is, therefore, threatened with further loss. If you feel that this kind of intervention is necessary, it is suggested that you consult with a professional first.

Trying to motivate someone to change through the use of guilt is also not helpful and potentially harmful. A natural consequence of depression is a destructive focus on feelings of guilt. Statements such as "You've got to pull yourself together; think of how it affects your family" or "We'll feel bad if you can't do it" only add more fuel to this destructive fire. Helping people who are depressed requires that you be willing to accept them where they are, and seek to assist them through rebuilding self-esteem rather than assaults on it through guilt trips.

Fears about Change

Some individuals fear and resist changing because they believe the concern of others will cease if they get better. They perceive their relationships with others as based on being taken care of, and even though they resent this feeling at times, they fear people will ignore them if they are well. Successful helpers try to communicate genuine concern and love during the whole process of recovery from depression and thereafter, too. They emphasize through words and actions that their caring for the individual is not based solely on the need for help.

Tom had suffered from depression for several years following his divorce. During this time he lived near two of his sisters, who were married and seemed to be quite happy and successful. They often invited Tom to join their family outings, but he told himself he was a failure because of his divorce and that his family was too good for him. When they tried to get involved with him, he thought they just felt pity for him. In the course of therapy, it became clear that Tom enjoyed his family but feared that they would lose interest in him if he did not need them because of his illness. He recalled times when he was doing a little bit better and then felt that his sisters were beginning to ignore him. Tom made lasting progress only when he discovered ways to be close to his family that were not centered around his illness.

Depression like Tom's, which lingers in spite of medical efforts and help from others, may be providing to the person what psychologists call "secondary gain." In cases like these, the illness has created some benefits for the individual that he does not know how to achieve in another way, and he therefore fears and resists change. Psychological counseling is usually necessary to resolve these fears and help him discover other ways to meet his needs.

Knowing Our Limits

Truly helpful people recognize when they have reached the limits of their abilities, and they ask for help themselves. Because we are human and our skills are limited, we are likely to encounter many situations where more expert help is needed. Responsible and prudent individuals seek help from professionals rather than trying to handle problems about which they are not knowledgeable. Suicidal individuals or people who threaten harm to others should always be directed to professionals for assistance. We risk damage to ourselves, as well as those we had hoped to help, when we go beyond the limits of our skills.

Marv was a conscientious, kind member of a ward bishopric and tried to help people whenever he could. Because of his willingness to get involved, people began to seek him out for counsel and assistance. Even after he was released from the bishopric, he continued to be available at all hours, if needed. Soon, however, he discovered that it was impossible to meet with people as often as they wanted or offer solutions to their serious problems; one young woman even threatened and attempted suicide several times when he could not see her.

Though his intentions had been good, Marv was caught in a discouraging and dangerous situation because he had taken on problems greater than the skills he had with which to help. His job, school, and physical and emotional health all suffered greatly, and some of the people he had wanted to help were delayed in getting the kind of assistance they needed because he did not recognize his limits. Marv eventually learned, through some difficult experiences, how to tell the difference between a "psychological tune-up" and a "major overhaul," and he found joy in helping when he could and assisting people to identify other resources when their problems were out of his range.

It is important for us to pace ourselves in the amount of time and effort we spend in service to others. Initially when we try to relieve depression, spending a little time assisting someone else can provide the boost we need. Trying to do too much, too soon, however, can lead to our becoming overwhelmed and even more depressed.

Tammy's bishop wisely suggested a number of small projects she could undertake for needy ward members that he knew they would greatly appreciate and that would, he hoped, improve her self-esteem. After a few weeks, she felt much better and wanted to get involved helping in other ways because she recognized the lift it had given to her. When the bishop suggested that she volunteer time at the genealogical library, Tammy was enthusiastic. She had long had an interest in this work but had not had the time to pursue it.

Some time later, however, Tammy began to feel overwhelmed again. She had volunteered to work at the library almost every day because she enjoyed it, but she had trouble doing this as well as trying to meet her normal commitments to her husband and family. She lapsed back into depression and became very self-critical, thinking that the reason she could not work as much at the library was her inability to manage time and her general incompetence. Eventually Tammy learned the importance of pacing herself. The old saying "too much of a good thing" also applies to service.

Sowing and Reaping

Peter clearly presented the eternal principle of giving and receiving when he wrote to the Galatians, "Bear ye one another's burdens, and so fulfil the law of Christ. . . . Whatsoever a man soweth, that shall he also reap. . . . Let us not be weary in well doing: for in due season we shall reap, if we faint not." (Galatians 6:2, 7, 9.) The benefits of living in accordance with this law are infinite and fall into two general categories: (1) the immediate lift we receive by stepping outside of ourselves to help someone else and (2) the potential long-term consequences of adopting an open and giving style of interacting with others.

Getting outside of their own thoughts and feelings is very difficult for most depressed individuals. A natural tendency develops in which increasingly greater amounts of attention are drawn toward themselves and their woes, which, of course, only leads to greater depression. As their focus of attention turns inward, their awareness of the outside world and the needs of others narrows and diminishes. In this state, they feel very much alone because they cannot see beyond themselves to others.

One way to break through this isolation is to force ourselves to give service to others. Through anticipating others' needs and interacting with them, we can forget our own troubles and hurts for a while. Giving of ourselves to others somehow feels good, too.

Disciples of Christ will try to adopt an open and giving attitude toward others to fulfill His challenge to love one another as He has loved us. (See John 13:34.) Through His example, Jesus personified the "sower of good seeds" among men. Though His efforts to show love and kindness to others were sometimes rebuffed and He was ultimately crucified, do you suppose He would want to change His message or style? Because we, too, live in this less than ideal world, we sometimes need to rely on faith that sowing the good seeds of kindness and understanding whenever possible is the best course of action. These seeds do not always flourish for us, but they increase the chances for a rich harvest. By adopting this style, we become a little more like the gods who govern through the power of love.

"Even the server of many must have his own pitcher filled," states an old and wise proverb. When our own reservoirs of love and energy are depleted, we have to plan ways to become refreshed ourselves. Though part of this need can be met through service, other activities and relationships that build us are also important. Many professional helpers, such as psychologists, psychiatrists, and counselors, experience burn-out, dissatisfaction, and disappointment when they focus too much of their energy on assisting their patients. If just giving to others were enough, they would probably be some of the happiest people among us.

Successful helpers try to strike a balance between being there for others and taking care of themselves. Even Jesus sought quiet times away from the demands and cries of the multitudes—in Capernaum, on the Sea of Galilee, and in the desert. He drew strength at times from His family, from His disciples, from angels, and from prayer to His Father.

Finding Ourselves Through Helping Others

A seemingly paradoxical relationship frequently exists between giving oneself and attaining personal growth and increased joy. A Primary song explains, "When we're helping, we're happy." It is as if giving to someone else, even when we feel that we haven't much to offer, actually ends up benefiting us too.

Investing ourselves in others is particularly helpful, though difficult, when we ourselves are depressed. It is difficult to become motivated to serve because we have decreased energy, and it is difficult to take the risk of reaching out because our own self-esteem is low. It is easier to follow the natural tendency to withdraw from others and to be concerned only with our own problems. Though some periods of depression are precipitated by too much attention to the needs of others, it does not mean that we must relinquish every commitment in order to feel good again. Regaining a realistic balance between serving others and caring for ourselves can help decrease depression.

Chapter 11

OTHER RESOURCES

Books are limited in their ability to transmit information and effect changes in the lives of their readers. While books may provide information on identifying depression and offer sound principles to cope with it, many people need more than reading this or any book to escape from their bouts with the blues.

If you have reason to believe your depression is biologically based, if your illness fits the description for manic-depression given in chapter 4, if you have seriously contemplated suicide, or if you have made an honest effort to help yourself by applying these ideas but have experienced little success, please seek professional help. Don't settle for only a partial solution. Now, more than ever before, professionals can help people to escape serious depression through therapy and, in some cases, medication.

There are many possible medical causes for depression, including chemical and hormonal imbalances, physical illnesses, interactions between medications, and vitamin or mineral deficiencies (such as iron). A medical examination to rule out these types of problems, or treat them if necessary, is important if you are to use the techniques discussed in this book with the greatest possibility for success. Though modifying your thoughts and actions can have a powerful positive effect on your mood, that alone cannot resolve physical problems.

Many people express unfounded and unrealistic fears about seeking medical help. They naively assume that avoiding a physical exam will prevent illness or disease, telling themselves, "What I don't know about can't hurt me." In reality, our moods are very much affected by our physical health, and ignoring medical problems may subject us to unnecessary depression.

We are fortunate to live in a time when so much is known about how to treat depression that is biologically caused. With this increase in real knowledge, however, has also come an increase in "miracle cures," "secret remedies," and clear cases of quackery. The "snake oils" of today have scientific-sounding names, but their usefulness in treatment has not improved. Because depression is a serious illness that affects many people and is increasingly brought to the public's attention, the charlatans and shysters are focusing increased energy on promoting unproven and untested ideas. It is common to hear and read of new "herbal" remedies or simplistic "breakthroughs" for curing depression. The best way to protect yourself from such scams and fads is to seek competent, professional help. If you doubt the recommendations of your doctor, seek a second opinion, but be certain that the person you choose is well qualified to evaluate your condition.

Counseling and Psychotherapy

Medications or other care provided by a physician are effective in some cases, but the chances for improvement in mood are greatly enhanced when these procedures are used in conjunction with therapy with a competent mental-health professional. Not all types of psychotherapy are equally effective in treating depression, however, and not all psychotherapists and counselors work well with the problems associated with it. Many types of therapy are available, and some are more successful in the treatment of depression than are others. You have a right to know what type of therapy you will receive and how its success compares with other treatments for depression.

Gather as much information as possible when choosing a therapist. Ask people you trust for their recommendations—your doctor, your bishop, or close friends, for example. If possible, talk about your options with people who have had first-hand experience with therapy and who have problems similar to your own. Names of psychologists, psychiatrists, and social workers are also listed in the telephone book. In most states professionals using these titles must be licensed and meet established standards of knowledge and experience. If you have any doubts about a therapist's credentials, contact the professional regulatory agency for your state.

Therapy also is available from many public and non-profit agencies. Trained professionals are found on the staffs of community mental health centers, counseling centers, and various other facilities supported through public money or charitable contributions. Because patients are charged for services on a sliding-fee scale, according to an individual's ability to pay, many people who have severely limited financial resources and/or no health insurance are able to receive help from public agencies. To identify what agencies are available in your area, check the phone book, call local government offices, or contact a local information and referral center.

Group psychotherapy is another option available in some areas from both private therapists and public agencies. It can often treat depression successfully and is frequently less expensive than individual counseling because the members, in essence, share in paying the therapist's fee. Of course, each person also shares the therapist's time and attention with other group members.

Once you have contacted a therapist, take the time to talk about your needs and expectations. Ask for information about his approach to treatment. Describe your specific goals and how soon you hope to accomplish them, and ask if they seem reasonable and realistic. During the course of treatment, provide your impressions about your progress, or the lack of it. If you become discouraged, say so; don't just drop out. It is common, even with the best of counselors, to experience frustration from time to time. Be open about discussing this before you give up. The relationship between the two of you will be a major contributor to your success in treatment; keep tabs on your thoughts and feelings and learn to express them.

Seeing a counselor is most likely to bring about positive change if you are willing to initiate and experiment with changes in your thoughts and behavior. Therapy is usually of little value if a person approaches it passively and just expects the therapist to "fix" the problems. An old joke makes this point quite succinctly: "How many psychologists does it take to change a light bulb?" "Only one, but the bulb must *really* want to change!"

Natural Helpers

Besides psychotherapy and medication, some non-professional resources, often overlooked, are available to assist and support you.

Some families are able to offer help and support to family members who are struggling with depression. Such assistance may come through verbal encouragement, including the depressed person in activities, or lending a listening ear when needed. Unfortunately, many depressed persons feel estranged from family and friends who might be able to help them. They are afraid or unwilling to ask for help, and family members feel confused by their withdrawal and do not initiate contact. A kind of stand-off occurs, which produces more estrangement and discouragement. Though it may seem risky, it is often helpful to reach out to members of your family and ask for assistance in times of need. Be explicit about how they can help you rather than hoping they will guess or somehow know how to help.

The Church has also established an organization that, when functioning at its potential, can act like an extended family and provide people you can turn to for counsel, support, or other assistance. In many areas, leaders are receiving training in counseling skills that help them to assist members as well as learning to recognize when consultation with a professional is needed.

Some persons find that it is easy to seek help from fellow church members or leaders because a relationship has already been established, they feel that they are worthy to ask for help, or they believe that it is important to solve problems using religious principles. In order to prevent misunderstandings and disappointment, try to be clear with yourself and those from whom you seek counsel about what you feel you need and why you have come to them for help. Of course, church leaders and members are likely to provide counsel that is focused around religious issues or teachings because that is the nature of their association with you. If you are afraid you might be turned off by this approach, it is best to be honest about those feelings from the beginning.

Some friends are close and intimate enough that they can help lift you when you're down. Though most depressed people avoid contact with others, friends are often willing to be a sounding board or to help provide a natural escape from your problems by getting involved with you in pleasurable activities. Relationships frequently become deeper and stronger when friends share their joys *and* sorrows.

Self-help Opportunities

In many communities, classes and seminars are offered by mental health professionals on how to manage depression, stress, and other common problems. Such classes can be very effective in teaching general psychological principles and strategies for change, as well as providing some structure or suggestions about how to implement these ideas into everyday life. Classes may be sponsored through mental health agencies, hospitals, community education programs, or community service agencies. They are often advertised by public-service announcements in the media, flyers in public schools, or posters in public places. Check around to discover where such classes are taught. If they are not available in your area, it may be possible to organize them by contacting community service agencies, mental health professionals, or groups that could act as sponsors.

Support groups of various kinds are available in many communities. If there is not one in your area that specifically focuses on depression, other groups may be of benefit and support if they address problems that affect you. The goal of such groups is therapeutic in nature, and they often focus on such topics as overcoming alcohol or other substance abuse, parent training and support, or recovery from serious physical or mental illness. To find out what groups are available in your area, call agencies that work with people who share these concerns.

Groups have also been organized to fill general social and psychological needs of a specific population, such as Parents Without Partners. They are usually listed in the yellow pages of the telephone book under headings such as "Associations," "Social Clubs," and "Social Service Organizations."

Suggestions for Further Reading

Several good books are available that teach principles similar to those discussed here as well as other related topics. The usefulness of reading, however, is closely related to a person's willingness to apply in day-to-day life the ideas presented in the books. Avoid getting caught in the trap of reaching for *another* book to solve a problem before you have really tried to use the ideas in the one you've just read. This enticing form of avoidance is likely to keep you frustrated, overwhelmed, and blue. Here are five books that I have found to be helpful:

Jonathan Livingston Seagull by Richard Bach (New York: Avon Books, 1970). This book, the fictional account of a seagull's struggle toward perfection, is an uplifting and thought-provoking story. The author's conceptions of perfection and how one grows toward it are remarkably close to LDS teachings.

Feeling Good: The New Mood Therapy by David D. Burns (New York: Signet Paperback, 1981). Dr. Burns discusses ways to change thinking in order to decrease depression and improve mood, and includes many specific suggestions to help readers apply these ideas to their lives.

Intimate Connections by David D. Burns (New York: William Morrow and Company, 1985). Dr. Burns discusses loneliness and the need for approval and attention from others. He provides suggestions about improving self-esteem and cultivating positive relationships with others.

How to Survive the Loss of a Love by Harold Bloomfield *et al* (New York: Bantam Books, 1976). This is a highly readable book on grief and the grieving process. It provides help for dealing with obvious losses, such as death or separation, and not so obvious losses, such as aging, moving, or other changes.

The Road Less Traveled by Scott M. Peck (New York: Touchstone, 1978). The author discusses issues common to depressed individuals, though this is not primarily a book about depression. The sections on self-discipline and the problems one experiences in trying to love others are excellent.

INDEX